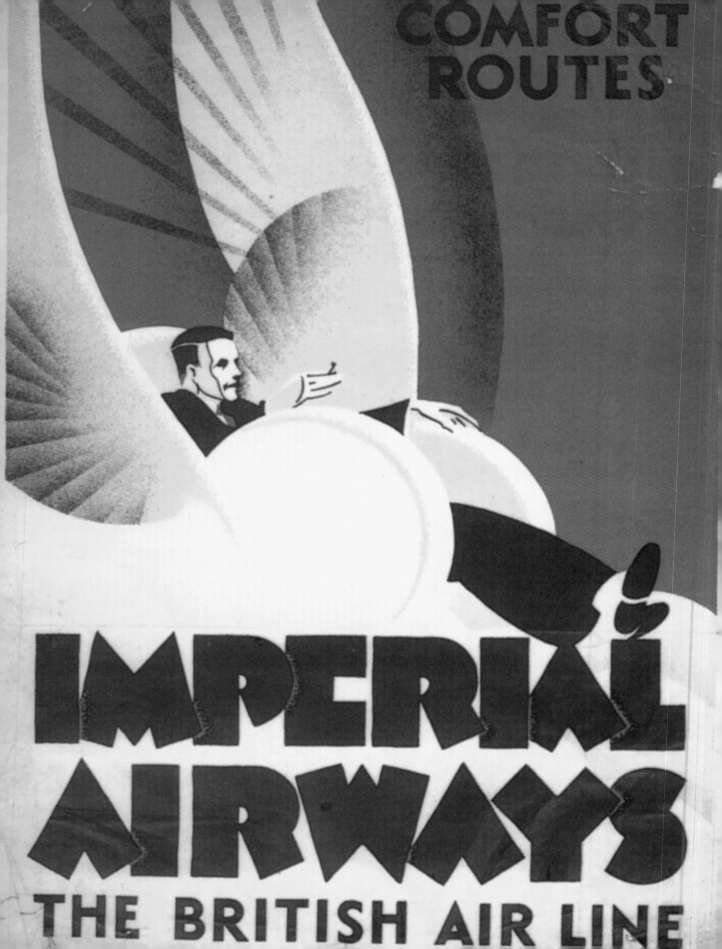

WINGS OVER THE WORLD

THE GOLDEN AGE OF AIR TRAVEL

Tom Quinn

AURUM PRESS
LONDON

First published in Great Britain
2003 by Aurum Press Ltd
25 Bedford Avenue, London WC1B 3AT

ISBN 1 85410 937 5

1 3 5 7 9 10 8 6 4 2

2003 2005 2007 2006 2004

Designed by Peter Ward
Printed in Singapore

CONTENTS

INTRODUCTION

Before the advent of the jet engine and the mass air travel it eventually made possible, flying was pretty much exclusively the preserve of the rich and powerful or for those whose work – the government, large corporations or the military – took them to distant countries.

Although passenger services were limited by today's standards there were scheduled passenger flights to the Continent as early as 1919 when Imperial Airways began services from Croydon Aerodrome. Later on there were also flying boat services from Southampton and then Poole Harbour, which flew stage by stage – and there were many stages – to the Far East and Australia or down through remote African stations to Durban or Johannesburg.

From the wider public's point of view, of course, passenger flying was still in its infancy even by the 1940s and it is difficult now to realise how different the experience of flying was then compared to flying now. Navigators still used what was in essence a sextant; aeroplanes could generally fly for only three or four hours before having to land; they flew low and slow and when they landed, perhaps at some remote outpost of Empire, the passengers on board dined with the flight crew and slept in the same hotel before continuing their journey in the morning.

Dining on board during the golden days of passenger flying was invariably luxurious silver service.

But if flying was slower in the 1930s and 40s than it is now it was also far more luxurious: before and after the War huge joints of meat were carved on board, passengers were served with the best china and silver cutlery by hostesses wearing white gloves; cabins were spacious and had bars at which passengers could smoke and drink. On flying boats passengers were invited to walk up and down on the promenade deck; there were cabins with beds, and a library. In the ladies' loos the most expensive cosmetics would be put out for passengers' use.

INTRODUCTION

2

All those early passenger planes – the huge Handley-Page HP42 biplanes, Armstrong Whitworth 10s, Britannias, Sunderland flying boats, Constellations and many others – are now museum pieces and there is only one way to return to that extraordinary vanished world of early passenger flying: through the memories of the men and women who knew it at first hand. Most are now in their eighties or nineties but as anyone who reads this book will quickly realise, their memories are pin sharp and hugely evocative of those pioneering days.

This is not, however, a book about the technicalities of flying. Inevitably it does cover many aspects of how early passenger planes were flown, but its primary aim is to discover what it really felt like to fly across the world when such an idea must have seemed breathtakingly daring to most people. It also looks at how pilots, navigators and other crew learned their craft and found their way into an industry that was new, exciting and at the cutting edge of technology.

In the early days, air travel seemed incredibly fast because most people were used to travelling – if they travelled at all – by boat. By today's standards, in contrast, early passenger flying seems almost as leisurely as earlier travel by ship. On a modern jet, passengers are packed in tightly and for the crew a journey halfway across the world doesn't mean a two-day rest in a good hotel, as it did forty or fifty years ago. Instead as often as not the plane turns round and comes straight back.

The complex teamwork that was once essential to passenger flying and the cameraderie of those pioneering days, the dangers of flying when no radio contact with the ground was possible, can be glimpsed again through the memories of the men and women whose stories form the basis of this book.

Here you will find the memories of men like Ron Ballantine, who flew with the great pioneering airman Alan Cobham just after the end of the Great War and later flew the present Queen back from Africa when her father died; or men like David Rose who was sent out to Africa to set up a flying boat station in the middle of nowhere; or Hilary Watson who began work as a steward for Imperial Airways in 1934 and later set up the first British passenger service to the USA; or women like Olive Carlisle ...

Here you will also find vanished trades – wireless operators, navigators and flight engineers – as well as accounts of historic flights culled from long out of print books; these include the extraordinary tale of Winston Churchill's first Atlantic crossing by flying boat, a crossing shrouded in the utmost secrecy.

Back in the days of Croydon Aerodrome, passengers had to be weighed as well as their luggage.

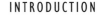

4

RON BALLANTINE
PILOT

When Princess Elizabeth's father died in 1952, Ron Ballantine was asked to fly her on the first stage of her journey from Africa as she returned to the UK as queen. It was the highlight of an extraordinary flying career that began when, as a boy of eleven in 1924, he flew with the great pioneering airman Alan Cobham.

Ron was born in Plymouth in 1913. His first great love was painting with flying a close second, as he explains.

'Well, flying was my second love until that first flight. We'd gone to see Alan Cobham, who was a well-known airman who ran something called a flying circus. Basically he went round the country stopping wherever there was a little aerodrome and offering to introduce people to the delights of flying – I remember you could choose a five-shilling ride or a ten-shilling ride. The more you paid the more time you got in the air. My dad paid for a five-shilling ride and it was so exhilarating. It was a little biplane, all canvas and wood and wire struts. I sat behind the pilot and held on for dear life – everything was open to the elements and there were no straps or safety belts.'

Still in love with the idea of being a painter Ron left Plymouth College at the age of sixteen and went to Plymouth School of Art. Flying was still running painting a close second, however, and by the time he went to art school Ron already had an A licence – a Royal Aeronautical licence.

'To get this privately you had to pay and learn to do a few circuits and what we called bumps or landings. I learned in a Klemm, a tiny German monoplane with a 30h.p. engine. It was really just like a glider. I was taught by an ex-RFC

Croydon Aerodrome in the days of
passenger biplanes.

RON BALLANTINE

Croydon Aerodrome's Plough Lane:
the runway was famous for its hump.

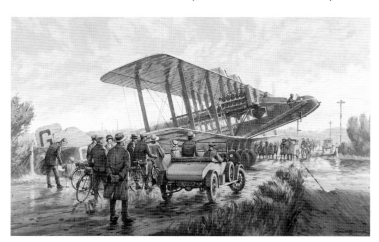

[Royal Flying Corps] chap who ran a flying school at Croydon and again my kind father paid the bill!

'That Klemm was difficult to control if there was much of a breeze and absolutely hopeless in a gale! I can remember the first time I went solo – I was absolutely terrified that I might break the plane. The instructor took me up two or three times and then just let me try it until I had enough confidence. I also flew a Gypsy Moth and a Puss Moth and then my first four-engined plane – a De Havilland 86 which was a biplane with four Gypsy Major engines. In any biplane flying is difficult in a gale because you have to allow for more drift. The controls were also rather primitive by modern standards on those little planes, held together with bits of string and wood and glue, but they were light and responsive to the touch.

'You had a trim wheel for nose heavy/tail heavy control, a throttle, an air speed indicator and an altimeter. There was also a control that we called a ball and stick – this was basically an instrument to tell you which way up you were flying! That might sound rather silly but it was actually quite important if you got into cloud where you might think you were flying level and actually be way off.

'Flying in cloud was always a little scary in those days – in fact when I later joined Imperial Airways the old World War I pilots I worked with hated blind flying. They would do anything to avoid it. I later did a blind flying course at Hamble where they took you up in a plane, put a hood over your head and then put your plane in a spin. With the hood on you then had to get out of the spin – it was good training but I can see why they use simulators for that sort of thing today! It was terrifying even though you knew that if you failed to

Cockpit of Imperial Airways' S-class biplane airliner *Scylla*.

sort yourself out the instructor was there to rescue you. I'd done that course long before any of those older World War I men could be persuaded to try it.' By this time Ron was so keen on flying that all idea of becoming a painter had gone. But the next change was to get a job in aviation and Ron wasted no time.

'I made a few investigations and went to see a Major Brackley, who was the Air Superintendent at Imperial Airways, to see if they would take me on.

RON BALLANTINE

8

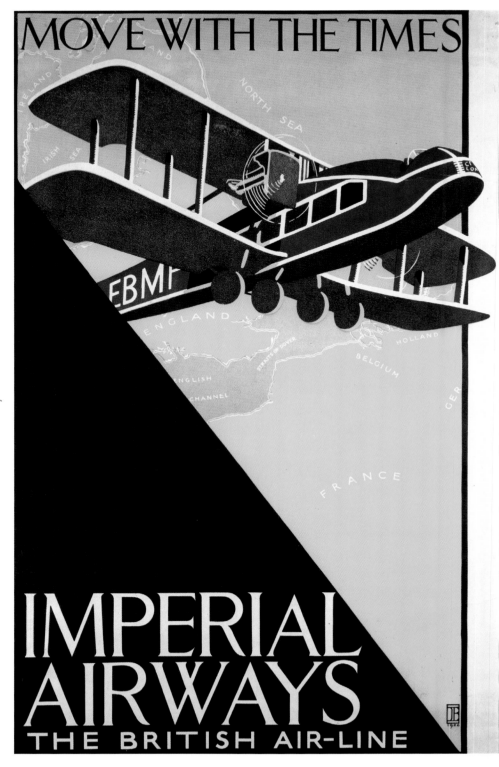

By this time I'd done so many courses that I had my B licence as well – this was a commercial pilot's licence. Major Brackley was interested but he told me to go away and get a wireless operator's licence. I went immediately to the London Telegraph School – nothing was going to stop me now – where I studied with lots of small boys learning to be marine telegraphers. The course lasted six months and I learned to do twenty words of Morse code a minute and I can still do it. In fact in odd absent-minded moments I still find myself tapping out messages! We learned on old Marconi equipment and a few Philips machines. On the planes these machines were installed behind the copilot. The Marconi machine was, as it were, the industry standard.'

After his six months' wireless operator's course Ron went back to see the Major at Croydon with his certificate and he was taken on as a probationary first officer. 'I spent the whole of my first year as a copilot to pilots who had learned their skills in the Great War. I hate to say it but some weren't very good pilots! Too stuck in their ways and rather slapdash sometimes.'

Ron flew with Imperial Airways on the only three passenger routes flown in the early 1930s – London to Paris, London to Cologne and London–Basle– Zurich. And without modern equipment and in low-powered planes without pressurized cabins the journey could be hazardous, as Ron explains.

'More often than not we flew in absolutely filthy weather with none of the electronic aids pilots have today. It is difficult to explain how lost you could feel up there when conditions took a turn for the worse – we had to navigate by landmarks. If you couldn't see anything on the ground you had a problem. As a copilot I couldn't do things my way but I had at least done my blind flying course. The pilots I worked with in the first year mostly had their own techniques for bad weather, though some had no technique at all!

'I remember once coming in towards Croydon Aerodrome with Captain O. P. Jones. There was so much cloud that we hadn't a clue where we really

Above: Imperial Airways Captain O.P. Jones.
Below: Flying in style: in the early days, passengers had masses of room and there were no safety belts.

were but flying just above the cloud. Jones, I later discovered, was searching for the tops of the two towers that then existed at Crystal Palace. He spotted the two spires just peeking through the cloud, turned to me and said, "Right, Mr Ballantine. Watch this." He lined up the towers, started his stopwatch, flew down through the murk and immediately before us was the aerodrome at Croydon. Jones was known as Captain Kettle, after the cartoon character, because of his beard!'

During these early years at Croydon Ron flew a number of biplanes – the Handley-Page HP42, for example, and the Armstrong Whitworth 10, which was a World War I plane still in use. It was a bomber converted for passenger flying. It had three engines but, according to Ron, was still incredibly slow. The HP42 – each individual aircraft had a name beginning with 'H', like *Hannibal*, *Hengist* and *Hanno* – carried twenty passengers; the Armstrong Whitworth, ten.

'We always had a steward to look after the passengers – this was long before stewardesses. In the cabin things were most luxurious because only the wealthy and important VIPs could afford air travel at this time. When people flew with Imperial Airways they enjoyed what was called the Silver Wing Service. This meant a big armchair and beautifully cooked food. The cabin was fitted out with

Air travel is more enjoyable by the largest air liners

The air liners of Imperial Airways are the largest in the world. Passengers are quick to appreciate the roomy great saloons, the stability in flight, the additional reliability of four engines, the full course meals with wines and liquors served by stewards, and the absence of noise. Then the Imperial Airways standard of personal comfort is unique and there are no irritating details like tips to worry you. That is why experienced Americans always make straight for Imperial Airways

| EUROPE | AFRICA | ASIA | AUSTRALIA |

IMPERIAL AIRWAYS

Bookings from Mr. P. E. Bewshea, Imperial Airways, The Plaza, New York. Telephone: Plaza 3.0794/1740 or from any Cunard White Star Office in the U.S.A.

overhead racks rather like a railway carriage and many of the fittings had mahogany or walnut veneer.

'On these passenger services we had two pilots – captain and first officer or copilot and originally there had also been a radio operator. Then after a while they got rid of the radio operator and the copilot did his work, which was fine for me of course as I'd done my six-month telegraphy course.

'Most of our passengers in the 1920s were regulars – we knew them personally. Men like the old Aga Khan, senior diplomats and military men.

The journey to Paris was two and a quarter hours and for people who were used to travelling by boat and train this was an extraordinary improvement – absolutely no one took it for granted because it was, as it were, at the cutting edge of technology.

'The pilot and copilot had identical controls, but some were duplicated and some not. The air speed meter and altimeter were only installed as part of the captain's controls.'

Croydon in the early 1930s was a bumpy grass field with just enough tarmac round the tower for the planes to line up and get a good run before they reached the grass, but as Ron recalls there was little room for error.

'There was nothing to spare on those runways. I suppose you had about 800 yards, which was tight – and I remember one chap flying a Velox didn't make it and hit the trees. But on a normal run you would never expect to do more than just skim the tree tops. The first time I did it I thought it was highly dangerous but of course you get used to these things. The airport buildings consisted of a tower and a central hall with counters on either side for the passengers to check in and make enquiries. Looked pretty much like a railway station with lots of dark mahogany. The tower was off limits to everyone except those with a special permit and all the planes were controlled using lights – there was no radio communication at that time. While the light was red you waited on that little patch of tarmac and as soon as it was green off you went.

'It may all sound rather basic and primitive but even then in the early 1930s a number of airlines flew from Croydon – Lufthansa, Sabena, Air France and of course Imperial Airways. London to Paris cost about £20, which was a lot of money in those days. Despite the fact that we all flew to the same places and you might think we would have got into a damaging price war, there were no subsidies and one imagines the companies involved made a good profit. Zurich was the furthest we flew.

'I did I suppose have what one might call a few near misses – fog was usually to blame. All you could do – like Captain Kettle – was try to spot a landmark of some kind and each of us had our favourites: it might be the spires at Crystal Palace as I've mentioned or the spire on Purley Ridge.

'I don't remember any real improvements in navigation until the second war had just about started – then we had sextants. In the late 1920s and early 1930s all we had was a drift indicator – this was a meter fitted to the floor and with a grid from which you could take a reading.

'Among my strongest memories of those early planes is the noise – I'm sure that's why my hearing is so bad now!'

RON BALLANTINE

12

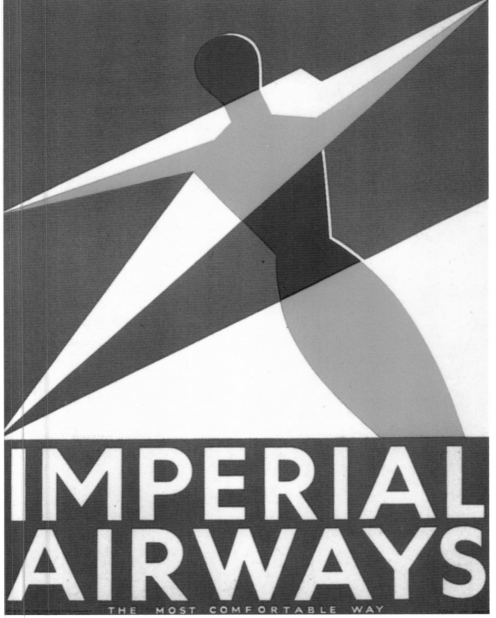

LE TOUQUET
ONE *FLYING* HOUR

IMPERIAL
AIRWAYS
THE MOST COMFORTABLE WAY

PILOT

13

Ron continued to work as a copilot flying from Croydon to the Continent until the 1930s when he was sent to India. 'Here I became a copilot on planes flying from Karachi to Singapore. But not long after arriving I was told that the pilot of a feeder line from Penang to Hong Kong had contracted malaria and I was given his plane and made acting captain. I took over the Penang to Hong Kong route. I was lucky to get that job at twenty-three because normally to be a captain you needed far more experience than I had at that time. Flying that route was terrible – there always seemed to be bad storms and coming in to Hong Kong was terrifying – you had to fly in through a narrow neck of water and once into that narrow neck you had to land whatever happened because it was too confined a space to fly out of again.

'By this time I was flying a De Havilland 86 biplane. I was being paid the princely sum of £250 a year plus two shillings and sixpence per flying hour because I had two licences, my B and C licences.

The Empress of Persia and her entourage about to board an Imperial Airways flight.

'It was extraordinary in those early days how there were absolutely no rules – I often flew eighty hours a week and later on did even more. You did what you felt like and no one said a word. I think that they knew you would be sensible. We flew till we were too tired and then the copilot would take over while you dozed. I came back to London from Singapore before the war – in 1938. During the first year of the war I flew to France with reinforcements. I also flew fighter crews and spare parts to Scotland and other bases. I was then sent to Nairobi to pick up an Atalanta, a four-engined monoplane we'd lent to East African Airways. I brought it back to England and then flew it on what were called reinforcement routes from Cairo to Singapore. We were flying government servants and businessmen and from time to time a VIP. I flew the Empress of Persia once and a number of ambassadors but hardly ever what you might call an ordinary person.'

When war broke out Ron found himself in Cape Town where he'd been sent to pick up a Lockheed Lodestar. Imperial Airways had bought several of the planes and Ron had been asked to take one back as far as Cairo.

'When I got to Cape Town I found the planes were all still in packing cases! I had to hang around for three weeks waiting for my plane to be assembled, but I had lots of fun because there were no young men around – they were being mobilized – and lots of girls!

'Once the plane had been put together I flew it to Cairo as planned and then flew troop carrier E-Class aeroplanes. When asked how many we could carry we always said about forty Gurkhas – being small we could get more of them in. I flew pretty much everywhere – all over Europe and Africa, Canada, South America and the Far East. The only place to which I never flew was Russia.

'The route to the USA was interesting – we flew from Prestwick to Reykjavik in Iceland and then down to St John's Newfoundland, Montreal and New York. During the war that route was usually OK, but flying from, say, Lisbon to England was far more dangerous – if there was cloud we'd stay in it over the Bay of Biscay where the Germans were always on the lookout. If it was clear we'd fly well out over the Atlantic because the Germans only had short-range fighters. The closest I came to getting into trouble was when I spotted a Heinkel, but I quickly found some cloud and vanished into it.

'The biggest change that the war brought to passenger flying – to all flying in fact – was radar. What a change that made! At last you had something that would get you through bad weather and enable you to avoid hills.

'Passenger services from Croydon to Paris continued I think until the fall of France, and Heathrow really came into its own after the war. The advent of Heathrow meant the end for Croydon, but for a while it was still used by small operators and for private flying as well as newspaper services. Imperial Airways became BOAC' (British Overseas Airways Corporation) 'early in the war, but the change had no effect on our work, although one thing I did notice was that when the company was privately owned people somehow seemed more enthusiastic. When we became state owned that enthusiasm seemed to diminish.'

Throughout the war Ron continued to fly troops, government officials and government documents around. When the war ended he found himself back in London. Then Hong Kong Airways, a subsidiary of BOAC, offered him a job as chief pilot.

'When I started with Hong Kong Airways they only operated locally and my job was to build the operation up, increase the number of destinations and so on. I was happy out in Hong Kong for two years and we expanded the routes to include the Philippines and Shanghai. I was flying a Lockheed Lodestar twin-engined plane again – I think of all the planes I flew that was the

most enjoyable. It handled so beautifully, was fast, well designed and comfortable for the passengers. We flew those at about 150mph an hour and when you compare that to one of the early biplanes I flew you'll realize what a long way we'd come. A biplane like the Hannibal would take off at 50mph because it had so much lift – but then it also had low-powered engines which meant it needed all that lift to have any hope at all of getting off the ground. Back at Gatwick in the early 1930s the old World War I pilots used to play about with the Hannibals if there was a bit of a gale – they'd rev the engines up and get into

Ron Ballantine (left) introduces his crew to Princess Elizabeth.

the air straight off the tarmac – a bit like a Harrier jump jet made of wood and string!

'After my two years flying as chief pilot based in Hong Kong I returned to the UK and flew Argonauts on all routes, which included two Royal flights – one to Nairobi and back on the Queen's accession in 1952, the second taking her and the Duke of Edinburgh to West Africa and back in 1954. I retired from flying with BOAC in 1966. In 1969 I was offered the job of Director of Flight Operations based in Singapore. I couldn't turn it down. In fact I enjoyed the job and did it until I retired from Singapore Airlines and came back to England in 1972, but some of the sparkle seemed to go out of life once I'd stopped flying.

'The highlight of my career was undoubtedly flying Princess Elizabeth from Entebbe to El Alamein, a night flight that took ten and a quarter hours. This was the first leg of her journey back to the UK and her coronation. I met her and she was enormous fun and very beautiful. She asked if I would fly around Mount Kilimanjaro so she could take a few pictures and I was happy to oblige. When we were coming in to land at Nairobi on the outgoing flight she asked if she could stand on the flight deck – I shouldn't have allowed it but it was terribly difficult to say no. If we'd had a bumpy landing she would have been thrown about and might have been injured, but I was very confident at that time and as it turned out we landed very smoothly and bang on time. She put her hat on and disappeared down the steps.'

PILOT

17

DAVID ROSE
STATION COXSWAIN
AND SENIOR STEWARD

Very few men alive today can claim that they set up an airport virtually single-handed. David Rose, who was born in 1924, did just that. In his early twenties he was sent to Africa to establish a stopping-off point for flying boats carrying passengers on the long journey from Southampton to Johannesburg. But how did it all start? As David, now a sprightly pensioner, explains, for him working for an airline back in the 1930s when he left school really had more to do with messing around in boats.

'Well, I was born near the coast – at Horton Heath near Wimborne in Dorset – and from as early as I can remember I'd always liked boats. All my friends had boats of one kind or another so when I left school at sixteen I knew that if anything turned up in the way of a job connected with boats I'd take it.'

The first job that David was able to find with any boating connections was working for the flying boat service – then run by Imperial Airways – that since early in the war had been operating from Poole Harbour.

'I jumped at the chance to join the old Imperial Airways Marine Section,' explains David. 'At sixteen it seemed an exciting job. The Marine Section was needed to operate the launches used to take departing passengers out to the flying boats and bring the arrivals in. You have to remember that they took off and landed about three-quarters of a mile out into the harbour. All the flying boats were C-class in 1940 when I started work – Imperial Airways' famous "Empire" boats, all individually named – there was *Caledonian*, *Cathay*,

Champion and so on. By now the war was on, of course, but despite many losses the flying boats kept flying — carrying cargo, mail and passengers. Some of the launches were detailed to carry mail and cargo, others were kept exclusively for passengers, others dealt with emergencies like a crash landing. And we had really fast launches that ran alongside the flying boats as they took off — the idea was that if there was a problem the launch would be alongside to rescue the passengers!'

David's first job was on what was called the rigger's launch. He spliced ropes and wires for the buoys that were used by the planes to moor up to after they landed. Flying boats were always tied up in the same way — as David explains.

David Rose (front) and fellow staff of the Imperial Airways Marine Section.

'When the flying boat had been secured and the passengers had been taken off and were heading by boat to Poole Quay the fuel barge would pull up alongside. Then the engineers went on board to do what we called the snags and refuel — that meant they were checking all the systems, the engines and equipment. The rigger's launch that I worked on would already have put a tail line on the back of the flying boat — this was a 4-inch diameter rope that was attached to a special hook under the back of the aeroplane and then run back to the buoy and made fast. It kept the boat steady while the engineers tested the engines. The tail line remained attached until the pilot — the skipper as we used to call him — pulled a lever when the aircraft was ready for taxiing. As soon as he did that the line dropped away.'

David joined Imperial Airways' Marine Section in November 1940 and what he remembers most clearly from those first weeks was the intense cold. The tail line might be dropped from a flying boat four or five times in a morning and each time it had to be picked up by the riggers.

'We went out in the launch and as I was the youngest member of the team I got the worst job — hauling the line hand over hand back into the launch. My hands got so cold doing this it used to bring tears to my eyes! And all the time I was breaking my back pulling that great heavy waterlogged rope in the cox

28
HYDRAVIONS 'EMPIRE' NEUFS
À VITESSE DE 320 KILOMÈTRES À L'HEURE
IMPERIAL AIRWAYS
EUROPE   AFRIQUE   INDE   EXTRÊME ORIENT   AUSTRALIE

Short Solent taking off from Cape Maclear, Lake Nyasa, Malawi.

would be shouting, "Come on, get a move on!'" – but despite these difficulties David loved the work and felt he was doing his bit for the war effort.

DAVID ROSE

22

'The war didn't change much for us – the flying boats were kept very busy throughout hostilities! But we started getting Sunderlands from the RAF' (the military counterpart of the Empire flying boat) 'as well as the usual C- class. Some of our lines to different parts of the world had been cut – they were just too dangerous – but many carried on regardless.'

After a year or so as a seaman David was promoted to second-class coxswain. That meant he occasionally escaped the rigger's launch to work on other boats including the engineer launches.

'Then just before I went into the Navy in 1942 I reached the dizzy heights of first-class coxswain. That meant I could take out the big launches – these were air-sea rescue boats and passenger launches.'

After call-up David joined the Navy and was sent to work on mine-sweepers. It seems that boats of one kind or another were somehow part of his destiny.

'We were officially the Royal Navy Patrol Service and a branch of the Royal Navy, but a branch that the rest of the Navy didn't like much! I think they thought we were just riff-raff! But minesweeping was dangerous work – many minesweepers were lost. When you caught a mine in your sweep you'd hear the wires sing as they got tighter and tighter. The idea was that the wire that tethered the mine under the surface would be cut by our sweep and the mine would float to the top. Floating to the top should have made it safe – that was the way they were built – but in most cases they weren't safe at all and if something just brushed the little horns at the top of the mine it would go off. If it was too close you'd get your arse blown off, as we used to say!'

The landing stage at Cape Maclear.

David stayed with the minesweepers until 1946 and then went back to his job on the launches at Poole Harbour. His job had been kept open for him, as was standard practice at the time, but when he returned he found that Imperial Airways had ceased to exist and he was now working for the British Overseas Airways Corporation – BOAC. By this time the flying boats had moved from Poole to Southampton. The route they took to South Africa was via Marseille, Cyprus, Cairo or Alexandra, Luxor, Cape Maclear, Port Bell, in Uganda on Lake Victoria, or Victoria Falls and finally on to Johannesburg. The whole journey took four or five days. Somehow his years at sea had made him restless and he decided he needed a change.

'I don't know what had got into me but when I got back to Poole Harbour I went to see the Senior Marine Officer – a Mr Smith – and told him I didn't want to work at Poole any more. I asked if there was any chance that I could work overseas. I was a first-class coxswain by now, and he told me there was a vacancy in Karachi. That sounded all right to me and one month later I found myself on the other side of the world.'

David spent his time working the launches for the flying boats at Karachi, Rangoon and Bangkok. Then he was sent to the then-Rhodesia (now Zimbabwe), to the station at Victoria Falls, for fifteen months, but he was enjoying life immensely, as he explains.

'I was young and single, everything was new and I loved it. I didn't mind where they sent me because it was all an adventure and as I was the only contract single bloke on the marine section I always seemed to be travelling. My unofficial title was Relief Overseas Station Coxswain.

'Planes only travelled by day, because they would have needed flare paths to land by and in Africa we couldn't put out flares – the hippos and crocodiles

would have swarmed around the light. After a night stop at the Victoria Falls Hotel passengers would get up at 6.30, have breakfast with the crew and take a bus from the hotel to the lake jetty. From here we'd take them out to the flying boat in our launches. They took off in the morning and landed in the afternoon – all very leisurely compared to today's flying. When they landed in the afternoon they'd be taken to their hotel for afternoon tea and then dinner.

'Throughout the journey down through Africa passengers got the sort of personal attention that would be impossible now. Most were service personnel or government officials. Private individuals were comparatively rare as only the very rich could afford to fly.'

When David flew out to India it was the first time he'd ever been in the air – apart, as he says with a smile, from one circuit at Poole and some bumps testing!

'On that occasion we were used as ballast. My strongest memory of those flights was the noise of the plane – and they were very noisy – and the fact that they flew so low, a maximum height of about 6000 or 7000 feet. On a clear day everything on the ground was clearly visible. When I flew out to Africa I remember the herds of deer and antelope running ahead of the shadow of the aeroplane.'

During his time at Victoria Falls David was sent occasionally up to Luxor on the Nile in Egypt, or Khartoum, where he heard that BOAC were going to operate a new service to Nyasaland (now Malawi) based on Lake Nyasa at Cape Maclear. No sooner had he heard the news than he was sent there to set up and open the marine side of the new station.

'I arrived at Monkey Bay, 10 miles by road, from Cape Maclear after a three-day journey on bush roads from Victoria Falls. I was with a colleague and on the last evening of the journey we took a corner too fast and turned the Land-Rover over. We had a couple of local youngsters with us and we asked them to go on ahead and tell the people waiting at Monkey Bay that we were going to be late because we would have to stay with the company vehicle. Their reply consisted of just two words: "No. Leopards!" So we sat in the jeep till dawn and then got a lift with a huge ramshackle Indian lorry.'

The new station on Lake Nyasa (now Lake Malawi) was to be at Cape Maclear. When David finally reached the lakeshore there was nothing – other than water – to suggest that this was a suitable place for a flying boat station: no buoys, no moorings or jetty, no offices or accommodation.

'We had to set up the station from scratch – we put a mooring down and as there was no proper buoy we used a 50-gallon oil drum as a buoy with a chain leading down to some old girders to anchor it in position. We had no

A tranquil scene: a BOAC Solent moored at Cape Maclear.

jetty in those days and no launches. We did have a small dinghy and that had to be used to get the passengers on and off the planes.

DAVID ROSE

26

'You have to remember that at this time this part of Africa was a British Protectorate and the Government wanted to open it up, to get trade in and out. Establishing a flying boat station was a start to this. After a couple of months the station was fully manned. Apart from me there was a station engineer, Mr Phillips; a radio officer, Johnny Harrup; and a traffic controller – Gordon Davidson, the station manager.

'The first aircraft came in just two weeks after I arrived. I was at the end of the landing area, which we'd marked out by now, in my tiny dinghy when Captain Magendy landed, taxied round and shouted from the cockpit window, "Where are the launches?" I had to shout back, "This is it, I'm afraid!" He just laughed. We rowed him and the passengers to shore in our little dinghy and then refuelled his plane from the one piece of equipment we did have by now – a small barge loaded with oil drums. Two hours after our first plane had landed he took off again for Johannesburg. This was on the Tuesday and on Thursday he was back again. We rowed the passengers ashore and those dis-embarking were taken by launch to Monkey Bay, which was about 8 miles from our landing area on the lake. Cape Maclear itself consisted of just one hotel, and they were taken from there by road to Blantyre.'

After several weeks using the little dinghy David and his team were told that a proper launch was on its way from Durban by rail, but it was due on the other side of the lake where the nearest railhead was situated. On the appointed day David went over in the little dinghy to collect the launch. But there was a slight hitch, as he explains.

'When I arrived at the railhead – the trains came from Mozambique – I saw the launch on a flatbed rail truck about 100 yards from the edge of the lake and I thought – how on earth are we going to get it in the water? We eventually went to a nearby village and managed to persuade the local lads to haul the launch over the sand to the water. We just about managed to get it there, but then had to wait for the wooden hull to plim up before we could tow it back to Cape Maclear! The whole thing had dried out while it was travelling and would have leaked like a sieve.

'Now we had a launch our next job was to build a jetty – something I'd never done before, but it was much easier than I'd imagined – just a matter of common sense really.

'The things I remember most from this time were the terrible mosquitoes and the long hours. I used to start work at five each morning and the week was split by the two flights I've mentioned – the flying boat that came in on Tuesday on its way to Jo'burg and then the same plane returning on Thursday.'

At the lake station David's routine was strictly adhered to.

'When we were expecting a plane we ran through the same procedures. We'd first make sure the appropriate area on the lake was clear of obstacles – that might involve going on a patrol in the launch to make sure there were no bits of driftwood floating about on the water. When the aeroplane was in range we would then radio and tell the captain where he should land – whether No. 1 area or No. 2 or whatever. Planes always landed into the wind with the launch running alongside as they came down and continuing alongside until the plane taxied to pick up a buoy.

'Very occasionally despite our best efforts to clear the water a plane would hit something on the water as it landed and this could rip the bottom out – thankfully nothing as serious as that ever happened during my time in Africa.

'People are often surprised to discover that flying boats could land easily on choppy water – even if the swell or the waves were really quite hefty the plane would still just come down and, as we used to say, kiss the waves before settling.'

Cape Maclear in the early 1950s
(top to bottom): the launch in dry dock;
passengers reach their flight; the local
BOAC team and engineers at work.

David stayed at Lake Nyasa until 1951. He hadn't been home on leave once in that time, but things were changing and the flying boat service was no longer economical. By 1951 flying boats were finished. One of the main factors was cost. All the overseas stations had been maintained by BOAC alone – this was very expensive but nothing could be done about it as no other seaplanes were flying. It was the advent of other aircraft – land-planes – that began to push down the cost of flying. And as other airlines took up the routes they were able to share airport fees.

'If I remember correctly,' says David, 'Pan American was the only other company with a flying boat service. We had three Boeing Clippers which flew from Poole to Shannon in Ireland and then on to Baltimore. Churchill always used this route.'

David resigned from BOAC in 1951 and came back to England. He tried various other jobs, including the Merchant Navy and then, in 1953, unable to resist the lure of flying, he rejoined BOAC as a steward on Constellations, Britannias, VC10s, Comets, 707s and Jumbos, retiring in 1972.

'That's how I met my wife – she was a stewardess. At that time there were just 200 women working as stewardesses for BOAC – there was a three to one ratio in favour of stewards. Stewardesses had to be able to speak two foreign languages and they helped with the meal service, although always under the male steward. The men still had overall responsibility for the bars and food. I remember flying to Rome on Argonauts. The journey took four hours and we served coffee and lunch. With fifty passengers, two stewards and a stewardess there was a lot more time to talk to people. The whole pace of the journey was extremely leisurely – when the Comets, the first passenger jets, came in, the London to Rome journey time was cut dramatically to just one hour and fifty minutes, but we were expected to do the same work in that time that we'd done in four hours before.

'Food was treated very seriously in the pre-jet era. The head steward, for example, would carve a huge joint of beef – there was no pre-packed lunch system. And that big joint of

Before the days of plastic meal trays, full roast dinners were cooked on board.

beef was cooked on board and served on china plates! Cocktails were also served – it all had to be in keeping with the fact that flying was a luxurious and expensive business.

'So far as we were concerned Heathrow airport in 1952 was just Building 221. That was where the crew checked in – but it was basically just a Nissen hut!

'Before we took off the bar steward had to go to customs to clear his bar and that bar stayed with him till journey's end even if that was twenty-two days later in Australia! When you landed in Rome, say, officials would take your bar – which was just a pile of boxes really – off the plane and put it in bond, in other words in a locked customs area. You only got the bar back when you flew on. And you couldn't open the bar until you were airborne.

'But it was a very exciting life – on the Australia run we'd go via Rome, Beirut, Karachi and Singapore, but we'd stop for two days in each place and stay in the best hotels. It was wonderful – I played golf all over the world and got paid for it! In Hong Kong we used to sail on a luxurious boat owned by BOAC.

'My strongest memories are of the noise of the Constellations – they were so loud you could never have a normal conversation while flying them. And then the astonishment when we flew VC10s – they were so quiet after the old props.

'I remember quite a few famous people too – Margot Fonteyn for example and Duncan Sandys. The stewardesses were always briefed about passengers in the famous Heathrow Building 221. They were told how many passengers there would be and whether there were any VIPs, any special diets.

'At the end of each flight as chief steward I had to fill in my report – I'd meticulously fill in what food we'd served, any remarks made by any passengers and so on. The stewardess also filled in a report. The idea was that if you were only working on part of the long journey to, say, Australia you could hand

SENIOR STEWARD

29

PREPARING LUNCH IN IMPERIAL AIRWAYS LINER "SCYLLA"

on your report to the next steward taking over and he'd be able to see at a glance what the various passengers were likely to want during the next leg of the journey. If they hated the steak or didn't like the cocktails we knew about it. So even if the crew didn't carry on with the plane your logbook did. And the report always ended up stored back in the office in London at the end of each journey. The reports would then be studied and you might be called to the office to explain something. It was all taken very seriously indeed. And as long as all the details of the journey were in your report you were covered.

'Amazingly, by the early 1950s there were already three BOAC services a week to Australia and three a week to Johannesburg. Food was loaded on freshly at each stop on the journey – except in Australia where we always had tinned food. During the 1950s too a lot of the passengers were emigrants – people leaving the UK and other parts of Europe to live in Australia, which was still offering thousands of assisted passages each year. We took an awful lot of people who couldn't even fill in their immigration forms, so the stewardess would go to the immigration buildings at Darwin or wherever (usually just a tin shed) and try to interpret for the new arrivals. We filled their forms in, but we always got it wrong – but the immigration officials couldn't understand the names anyway so eventually they would just give up trying to work it all out and let them through.

'Darwin was a terrible place then and I'm sure the local Australian officials felt they'd been sent there as a punishment! I remember it only had one hotel, Fanny Bay Hotel, and that was next to the prison – each day they would let the prisoners out to provide customers for the hotel. The hotel was run in a pretty eccentric way too – at seven each morning a girl would stand outside your room and shout, "You've got to get up!" and whatever else happened she wouldn't go away until you had got up. Breakfast too was an odd business – there was just one thing on the menu – kidneys, liver, fish and steak, and you had to have all four on the same plate.

'As chief steward I went to Australia two or three times a year, a couple of times to Singapore, twice to Tokyo and twice maybe to Johannesburg. Apart from checking the passengers and letting the captain know the tally, the chief steward would check the safety equipment, make sure all the food and drink was aboard and then close the doors before take-off. There were no intercoms in those days so the captain had to be told everything in person.

'The other thing that sticks in my memory is the fact that almost everyone smoked in those days. Air conditioning started to come in just before the jets arrived on the scene. That got rid of one of the major discomforts of flying. If we had to stop for any length of time at Bahrain or Karachi or anywhere really hot, the temperature inside the plane would soar within minutes. All we could do at the time was hand round icy towels. What a relief it was when airport air conditioning came in and we could plug the aircraft in at least while it was on the ground!

'Aircrew were always playing tricks on each other – putting soup in sick bags and pretending to eat it, or when we stayed in a hotel someone would set a rumour going that if you wanted someone in the night you should hang a towel on the doorknob of your bedroom. By midnight every single door in the hotel would have a towel hanging on it!

'But by the time I retired in 1972 and we were working on Jumbos the number of cabin crew had increased from four to fourteen and after we landed everyone would vanish. The days when we all stayed together were long over.

'In all my years of flying I had only one incident – we were flying into Tehran on one of the early Comets and I thought, "That's funny – we're a bit high up" – then before I could think, we dropped the last 40 feet like a stone and skidded. We'd hit an air pocket right above the runway. The chutes all came out on stopping. That was frightening but not as frightening as when lightning used to hit the aircraft – it happened pretty frequently and there'd be a loud bang that sort of ran all the way along the plane.

'When I started flying the world still seemed a pretty big place. Then, as the planes got bigger and faster the world seemed to shrink. But living out of a suitcase is addictive. When I retired it took me ten years to get used to the fact that it was all over. It was I suppose what you could call a champagne existence on a beer allowance!'

SENIOR STEWARD

31

GOING TO COLOGNE

Suppose we are going to Cologne. By 'surface travel' it will take us eleven-and-a-half-hours via Dover–Calais or Dover–Ostend, thirteen hours via Harwich–Flushing, or fifteen hours via Harwich–Hook of Holland. But by Imperial Airways we can reach Cologne airport from Croydon in less than three hours, or including coach journeys to and from airports, the heart of Cologne from the heart of London is only four hours distant.

At the London Airways Terminus we are weighed with our baggage – and passengers sensitive about their weight are relieved to discover that only the official behind the counter can see what it all comes to! The baggage has distinctive Imperial Airways labels affixed, and we see it no more until Cologne is reached. Outside, a comfortable Imperial Airways coach awaits us, and soon we are speeding through South London suburbs to Croydon Aerodrome. We catch a glimpse of machines in the air and on the ground as we turn into the approach to the airport buildings; but it is not until we have gone through the passport examination and stepped out on the tarmac that those of us who have never seen them before at close quarters, realize the size and power of the machines used in air transport today, and the numbers of different air-lines using the airport.

The passport examination is very different from those we have known and loathed. There is no waiting in long queues of weary and disgruntled

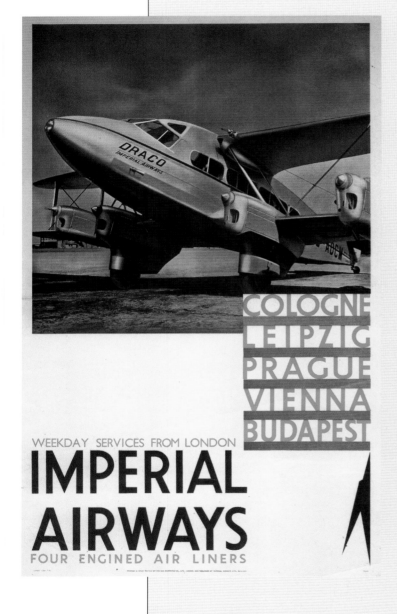

COLOGNE
LEIPZIG
PRAGUE
VIENNA
BUDAPEST

WEEKDAY SERVICES FROM LONDON

IMPERIAL AIRWAYS

FOUR ENGINED AIR LINERS

32

travellers in ramshackle and draughty buildings, or even in the open air. We are 'few at a time', we hand our passports to the officer, who soon returns them, and we pass the keen eyes of the inevitable detectives without knowing, in our innocence, that such people are there at all.

At the departure point on the 'apron' stands *Scylla*, the shining four-engined monster that is to fly us to Cologne. It is a fine bright morning, so we really have no need of the long cov-

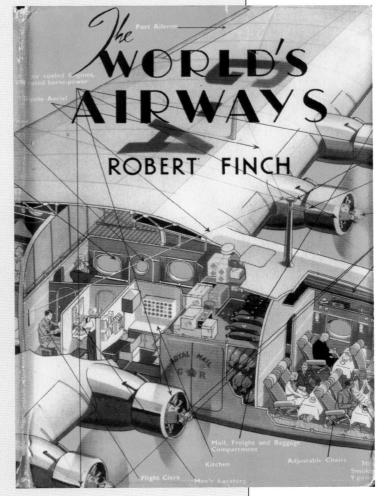

ered way that is wheeled up for us between the hall and the door of the aeroplane; with its raised head over the steps which give access to the door it looks very much like a bloated caterpillar – indeed, I believe it is irreverently called by that name.

Scylla has an astonishing amount of room inside. Her inner walls are panelled with fine polished woods; her furnishings are luxurious. She can carry thirty-two passengers in addition to her crew of five. She is equipped with all arrangements for passengers' comfort – including a kitchen from which meals and refreshments are served by a smart steward during flight. Many air travellers have happy recollections of complete lunches from soup to coffee on board *Scylla* – deftly and promptly served without any of the disturbing incidents common at meals on some fast express trains.

Looking forward we can see the entrance to the pilot's cabin – the 'bridge', so to speak, of the ship, but commonly known as 'the office'. It is remarkably roomy in comparison with the somewhat cramped quarters on many fast modern machines.

Now the powerful engines begin to turn over. The panel on the parapet of the Control Tower shows in white on its green background our initial letter: it is time for us to move off. The pilot in charge taxies *Scylla* to the far lee side of the aerodrome and faces her to the wind, his engines at low throttle, his eye on the Control Tower. Suddenly a powerful beam of white light is projected onto the machine; it is the signal to start. A touch of the pilot's hand and the engines open out with a deep roar as *Scylla* runs up into the wind with ever-increasing speed until she is away. It is impossible for a mere passenger to tell the exact moment at which she leaves the ground and becomes airborne. There is no sense of insecurity; we feel as comfortable as if we were in a good, fast car, and can look out and down through our wide windows at England sliding away beneath us. Now and then we feel the powerful urge of the propellers as we gain height; but there is remarkably little noise, and conversation can be carried on in ordinary tones quite as easily as in a fast train or car.

The fields and orchards, pastures and woodlands of Kent pass in intricate patterns beneath us. Brown and black roads crawling with beetle-like cars, shining sheets of water and gleaming streams, long curves and straights of glistening railway lines are there too. It is not until we see our shadow leaping swiftly over hedgerow and field, and easily outstripping the fast trains to the coast, that we realize the speed at which we are travelling.

Fleecy balls of cloud sail along around us, soft and white as carded wool.

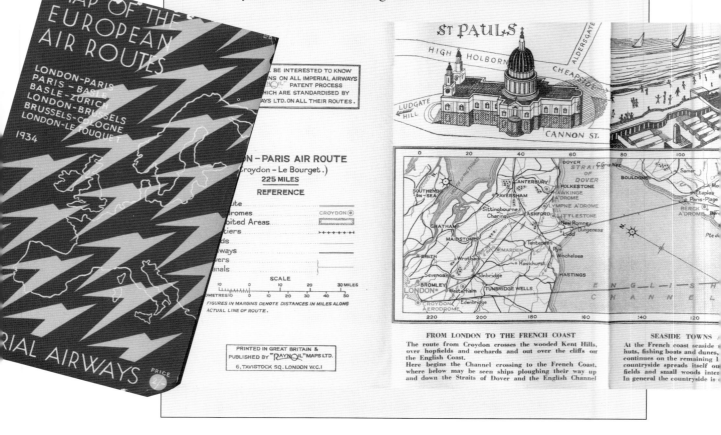

FROM LONDON TO THE FRENCH COAST
The route from Croydon crosses the wooded Kent Hills, over hopfields and orchards and out over the cliffs on the English Coast.
Here begins the Channel crossing to the French Coast, where below may be seen ships ploughing their way up and down the Straits of Dover and the English Channel

SEASIDE TOWNS
At the French coast seaside huts, fishing boats and dunes, continues on the remaining countryside spreads itself ou fields and small woods inter In general the countryside is

Sometimes a mist-wreath envelops us and we see the ground in sunlit patches through it. As *Scylla* enters a larger white cloud than usual, she gives a sudden lift, not by any means unpleasant, as she is borne aloft on the up-current of air at the cloud's edge; and when she emerges there is a slight downward movement as if she were taking new breath for greater speed.

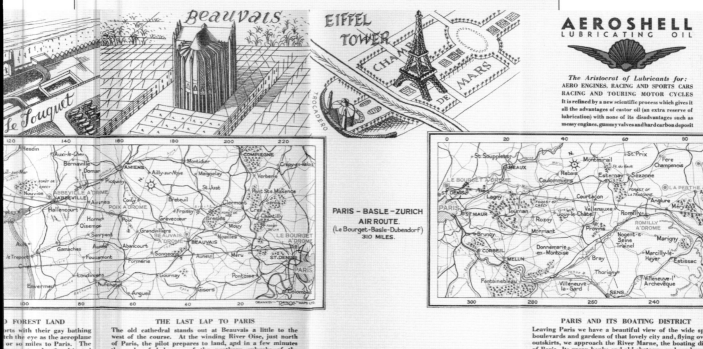

Our course is set eastwards and a little south of Maidstone, and in an incredibly short time we see ahead a pretty seaside town spread like a coloured map before us – its open suburbs, its heart of closely packed buildings, its promenade, its strip of yellow sand and its pier stretching out an absurdly small distance into the sea. Hardly have we called one another's attention to it than we are over the Channel, which on this fine morning looks from a height like a vast spread of pale blue and green shot silk. A glance at the altimeter dial beside the clock in our cabin shows that we are flying at 4000 feet and still ascending.

Down there, suddenly, is a long and ragged patch of yellow sands fringed on the windward side by vivid white lines of creaming surf – the Goodwin Sands, visible above water at low tides. We can see them extending beyond the

PARIS – BASLE – ZURICH
AIR ROUTE.
(Le Bourget-Basle-Dubendorf)
310 MILES.

D FOREST LAND
orts with their gay bathing
tch the eye as the aeroplane
or so miles to Paris. The
n a network of cultivated
rsed with villages.
little interest on this sector

THE LAST LAP TO PARIS
The old cathedral stands out at Beauvais a little to the west of the course. At the winding River Oise, just north of Paris, the pilot prepares to land, and in a few minutes the red-roofed houses of the northern suburbs of the capital pass beneath the wings, and there ahead are the large hangars of Le Bourget

PARIS AND ITS BOATING DISTRICT
Leaving Paris we have a beautiful view of the wide spaces, boulevards and gardens of that lovely city and, flying over its outskirts, we approach the River Marne, the boating district of Paris. Its green banks and old chateaux and gardens right at the water's edge offer a delightful view and the wooded country between here and Romilly is very picturesque

35

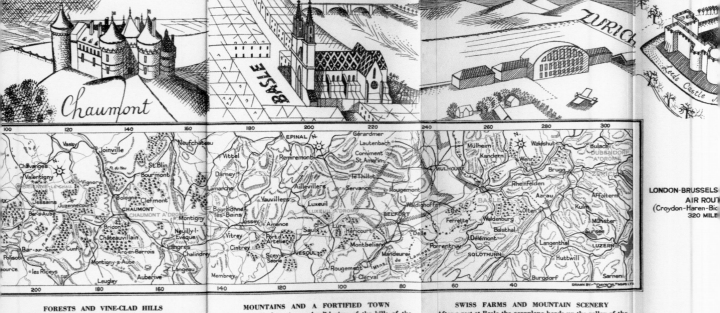

white of the surf in long undersea peninsulas that become less and less defined as they reach deeper water. At 6000 feet, and halfway across to the Belgian coast, we pass over the *Prince Baudouin*, the crack vessel of the Belgian State Railways, on her way from Dover to Ostend. We can tell from the wide V she is spreading, and from the long wake she leaves astern, that she is making her usual 21 or 22 knots; yet she seems to be still – and so very much like a tiny toy.

Now as we reduce height, the water shallows – we can see the sandbanks beneath it – as we approach the long flat sandy shores of Belgium with popular watering-places, of box-like hotels and houses strung along a yellow shore dotted with basket chairs and bathing huts and speckled with bathers. Presently we are over a land as flat as a pancake, in places cut up by the thin lines of many canals. In others divided into intriguing geometric patterns of green, yellow and brown fields, edge to edge like the patterns on some modern carpets, without any bordering hedges and only occasionally a long line of tall thin trees marking a thin straight road or canal, or a clump around a village or farmstead.

FORESTS AND VINE-CLAD HILLS
Soon after Romilly the valley of the Aube meets that of the Seine and we fly along above the junction of the two and arrive over Brienne with its white chateau on the central hill. After this the ground rises and there are large forests on each side. We continue above thick forests and again cross the Marne near Chaumont, which is a famous wine district

MOUNTAINS AND A FORTIFIED TOWN
After Luxeuil there is a splendid view of the hills of the Vosges and we now turn towards the fortified town of Belfort where higher mountains begin. There is a stretch of wonderfully fertile country as the Rhine is approached, and a forest on the left, and then the clean and well-built town of Basle is reached at a turn in the river

SWISS FARMS AND MOUNTAIN SCENERY
After a rest at Basle the aeroplane heads up the valley of the Rhine with the mountains of Germany on the one hand and the Jura Mountains of Switzerland on the other. The Bernese and Engadine Alps can be seen to the right, and we fly over farms and fertile slopes, with streams and waterfalls below, before the lake and Airport of Zurich are reached

Suddenly below us appears a river winding in intricate bends. It is the Lys, whose waters are ideal for retting the flax grown down there; those white patches looking like washing laid out to dry are strips of linen bleaching in the sun. Steepled towns with high-pitched roofs and wide marketplaces swing away from beneath us; villages, too, at cross-points on the spiderweb roads that feed the market towns radiating from them like spokes from the hub of a wheel. At last, beyond the windings of the Escaut (Scheldt), the dark mass of Brussels resolves itself into a city of fine buildings and busy streets as we circle down over the Royal Palace to the Haren Airport and come to earth as lightly as a bird.

Soon we are off again, heading by way of Louvain directly for Cologne. The country seems much more wooded. Towns and villages seem more frequent, the architecture is different and roads are wider. Now factories and works appear as we pass over part of Belgium's 'Black Country'. The crossing of the winding Meuse takes us for a little over a piece of Holland – the long south-projecting strip of Dutch Limburg. Then comes Germany, with fields of different patterns from those of the Low Countries, with more works and

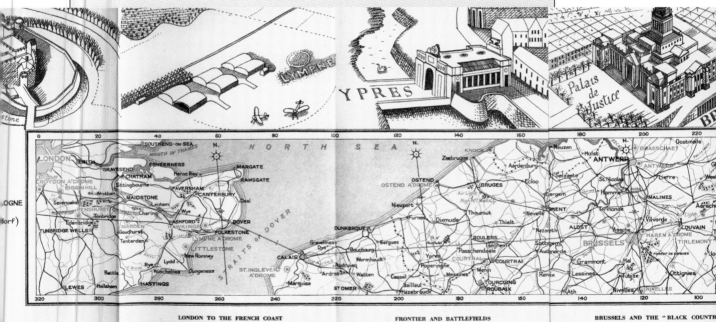

LONDON TO THE FRENCH COAST
Leaving Croydon the airliner turns South-East for the coast. Sevenoaks and Maidstone are soon passed over, and a moment later Leeds Castle, situated on an island in the middle of a beautiful lake, comes into view
Before leaving the coast at Dover, the market town of Ashford can be seen, followed by the R.A.F. Aerodrome at Hawkinge, near Folkestone. Soon the white cliffs of Blanc Nez are seen on the right, before the airliner reaches Calais

FRONTIER AND BATTLEFIELDS
After Calais a course is set for Brussels. Dunkirk is noticed on the left, and the airliner passes immediately over the town of Bergues, whose fortifications are of outstandingly geometrical design
After passing the Franco-Belgian frontier a complicated structure of waterways indicates the Yser canal system. Soon we are over the shell-battered Houthulst Forest, and later over the town of Roulers, which has been practically rebuilt since the end of the Great War

BRUSSELS AND THE "BLACK COUNTRY"
We now cross two noticable rivers, first the Lys, with its twists and turns, and then the Escaut. After this the airliner reaches Brussels, the first port of call, and after flying North almost immediately over the magnificent Royal Palace of the Belgians, lands at Haren Aerodrome. Leaving Brussels after a brief halt we approach Louvain and presently the great industrial district, the *Black Country* of Belgium

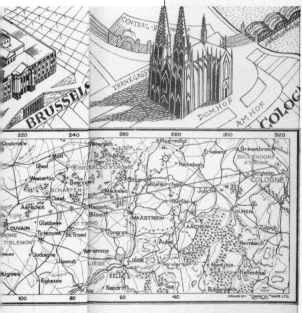

quarries, factories and towns. At one point we pass very near large open coal-workings with iron foundries close by. Next we get a glimpse of Aachen and of tall chimneys of white cement, ironworks and steelworks and factories without number. At last the Rhine! And by it Cologne, unmistakable owing to the magnificent landmark of its twin-spired cathedral and its fine river-bridges. We circle down to the Butzweiler Hof Airport, and in a few minutes are passing the usual Customs and Passport examinations. Again, there is no fuss; everything is conducted quickly and quietly with welcome politeness and consideration. In a remarkably short time we are in the bus that conveys us swiftly to the Dom Hotel under the very shadow of the great cathedral itself and in the very heart of Cologne. A journey which would have taken us about twelve hours by any other means has been performed with extreme comfort in four.

The World's Airways, Robert Finch, 1938.

INTO HOLLAND AND GERMANY

Next the River Meuse is crossed and for a short time the airliner flies over the small piece of Holland that projects between Belgium and Germany. Soon we are over the frontier and in Germany, and presently see the Cathedral of Cologne with its twin spires, grotesque with their numerous points. In a few minutes we land at the Airport of Cologne

...CK COUNTRY"
...the Lys, with its innumerable
...fter this the airliner reaches
...er flying North of the City,
...a Royal Palace of the King
...ne. Leaving Brussels after a
...esently the great industrial

SEE EUROPE IN COMFORT BY AIR!

Lunching in the air
between London & Paris

Imperial Airways offers the most distinguished and exclusive means of travel in Europe. Its air liners are the most luxurious in the world and individual attention is paid to passengers in a way which is unknown in surface travel. On the main European routes of Imperial Airways, one or more stewards are carried in every air liner. Appetising meals are served during flight and there are armchair seats for every passenger. There is at least one lavatory in every air liner and plenty of room to move about freely

From London you can fly to Paris while you lunch, to Brussels and Cologne after lunch, and during the summer to Le Touquet for the week-end, and to Switzerland in half a day. There are connexions by air from these places to most of the principal towns in Europe

IMPERIAL AIRWAYS

THE GREATEST AIR SERVICE IN THE WORLD. Bookings and information about Imperial Airways travel from Mr. P. E. Bewshea, Imperial Airways Ltd., The Plaza, Fifth Avenue and 59th Street, New York. Telephone: Plaza 3 [0794 1740

Stuarts.

VIC AVILA
PILOT

Victor Valentine Avila was born in 1923 in Essex and first flew when he was five. Against all the odds he was to become a pilot, flying first with the RAF and then with British European Airways – BEA – from Northolt. But his love of flying began with a five-shilling ride in 1928.

'I can remember holding on tight in this tiny open cockpit with my mother and seeing the wind from the propeller knock my dad's hat off as he stood behind the plane watching. As the engine revved up I shouted, "Down! Down!" and the plane hadn't even taken off! I can remember that plane was piloted by a chap called Neville Browning who farmed near us' (at Navestock in Essex).

Vic's uncle was a pilot, so in a sense flying was in the family, but more immediate family difficulties meant that Vic had to leave school at fourteen to earn his keep and with so little education he knew that becoming a pilot was now going to be extremely difficult.

'I had to leave school to help support the family. So I worked in a factory (Chris Cottice's Iron Foundry) in Epping, drilling holes! I did that for a few months and then got a job in the Lee Valley growing greenhouse tomatoes and cucumbers but all the time I knew I wanted to fly. At fifteen I left home and lived in digs supporting myself and nurturing my dream.

'Eventually I got a job with a tractor firm, Jack Oldings Ltd Caterpillar and John Deere Tractors of Hatfield, which later dealt with Stuart Lee Grant and Sherman tanks – we serviced and overhauled them. We used to drive them along the local roads at up to 40mph terrifying the locals. A Sherman tank at 40 is quite a sight! But I learned about engines and it was particularly helpful as the American tanks were fitted with Pratt and Whitney Single and Twin Wasp aircraft engines.'

Vic stayed at the tractor factory till he was eighteen and then applied to join the Air Force. He was turned down flat simply because of his lack of schooling.

'That was in 1940, but I bet I knew more than anyone else my age about how engines worked, as well as the Caterpillar tractors. I knew every nut and bolt in those tanks, particularly the ones fitted with aircraft engines!'

Vic refused to give up after being turned down by the Air Force. But the difficulties he faced in achieving his ambition were if anything greater now than they'd ever been. Then luck gave him his chance.

'Well, I knew that at Hatfield – the aircraft manufacturer De Havilland's base – there was an RAF unit so I simply went along and asked if it was possible to get any tuition with maths, navigation and so on. While I was making my enquiries I was introduced to a wonderful chap called Leslie Green who was working nearby as a nightwatchman. He'd been a pilot in the Great War, but had been badly injured. He could have been a brilliant teacher but he was so poorly that even teaching was too much for him. I was told that he might be able to help me get into the Air Force, and out of the goodness of his heart and for no financial reward he agreed to help me. At this time I also joined the Air Training Corps. I was determined to do everything I could to improve my chances of being accepted second time round.'

Vic now found himself working in the tractor and tank factory five and a half to six days a week, from seven in the morning till five at night, and then spending several hours each evening with his volunteer tutor.

'Mostly he taught me maths and English, which were essential if I was to pass the rigorous RAF Pilot Entrance exams,' explains Vic. 'Leslie was a remarkable man – tall and distinguished-looking. He had no family and lived quietly in digs. He was very well educated – fluent in French and German – but also knew a lot about the ins and outs of the Air Force.

'So I spent many months working all day and then spending my evenings from seven till perhaps eleven working with Leslie. He asked me right at the beginning what I wanted to do. I told him it had to be a pilot – no other aircrew job would do because my occupation was reserved which meant I needed a very good reason to leave it and join up. If they needed me as a pilot that would do the trick. I probably worked with Leslie for eighteen months in all. He knew I was absolutely dedicated and single-minded. I wanted to fly because in a sense I had nothing and it was a way to escape that situation.'

Vic applied to join the Air Force a second time. He sat the exams and the

panel asked to see him. They were by all accounts astonished. They knew he'd left school at four-teen yet he'd almost achieved a perfect 100 per cent mark — it was unheard-of.

'I told them that this was the second time I'd applied and that if they turned me down I'd only apply again. But that was enough for them and at last I'd achieved my ambition. It is difficult to say how pleased I was because all the other young men who'd been accepted had been at grammar school till they were eighteen or they had university degrees.'

The factory owners — Vic's employers — were not very happy when he told them he was leaving to join aircrew — 'I think they felt it was only something for the well-to-do, the sons of factory owners. It was not for people who worked in factories!'

When Vic was finally called up a few months later he found he was the only person on the course who'd left school at fourteen, but he was already ahead of the game. 'We were sent to Brighton to learn maths, navigation and Morse code. Well, I'd already taught myself Morse code in the factory — I'd found an old buzzer and used to tap out messages in any spare moment.

'I knew my training would be the best in the world and stand me in good stead for any kind of flying — military, passenger, freight, whatever.'

Vic was sent to Aberystwyth University's Initial Training Wing where he passed all his exams. He then went to Worcester for the statutory twelve hours' flying.

'We went up in a Tiger Moth with a pilot instructor. There was no mess-ing about in those days — you were expected to go solo in twelve hours. If you failed you were out.

'After that we went through a selection procedure to sort us into pilots and navigators. I've often wondered what on earth I would have done if at that stage I'd not been selected as a pilot — anyway the problem didn't arise because I was selected as a pilot and I was sent to Manchester, then Glasgow, and then on the *Queen Elizabeth* to Halifax, Nova Scotia.'

Despite the war the *Queen Elizabeth* was unescorted for the simple reason that she was too fast to be at risk from German submarines. In Nova Scotia Vic flew Fleet Finches — small biplanes with five-cylinder radial engines and a very narrow undercarriage.

'The narrow undercarriage meant that it was very difficult not to ground-loop the plane — that meant tip it over on one wing. In fact I was the only person among my colleagues never to ground-loop a Finch. They were elderly

ALL OVER THE WORLD B·O·A·C TAKES GOOD CARE OF YOU

planes but interesting to fly – the main thing I remember about them is that they had wooden propellers and wings made of canvas and string. We were the very last course to use Finches – they were just too old and constantly leaked oil.

'They took off at just 45–50mph and by today's standards their controls were very heavy, but they could still do loops, rolls and rolls off the top. The lack of power was the biggest problem – unless you were in a dive they'd barely do 100mph. Some didn't even have a proper air speed indicator – just a piece of metal with a spring on it! The faster you went the further back the spring went and you read your speed off from a mechanical scale.'

From Finches Vic quickly moved to Avro Ansons, a much more powerful twin-engined plane that could carry a few passengers.

Vic receives his wings after successfully completing his pilot training in Canada.

'I suppose that's where my passenger flying began,' he says. 'They had been used early in the war for patrols, but we used them to learn about instrument landing and for practice runs for bombing. By early 1944 I had my wings, but there were too many pilots by now so they kept us on till I think we were really trained to a higher standard than previously required.

'Claresholme, Alberta, where I was now based, was an interesting and demanding place to fly – it was 2000 feet above sea level with the Rocky Mountains to one side. We often had to land on snow and some people never got the knack of it – they tended to make heavy landings, which was always a bad thing.'

Vic was one of sixty trainees and of that number twelve were commissioned.

'In England with my background I would undoubtedly have been made a sergeant pilot – i.e. not an officer. In Canada the old school tie counted for nothing and on the basis of my ability I got one of those twelve commissions. So two years from being accepted as a pilot I was a pilot officer. Some of my colleagues complained bitterly about this – they didn't like the fact that I had been granted a commission when I hadn't had their education.'

Having completed his training Vic volunteered next to go to Pat Bay, Vancouver Island to train on Dakotas for Transport Command moving passengers and freight.

'At first we only flew military passengers and we flew them on Dakotas and Expediters, but we were still learning – I was still being sent on astro-navigator and radio courses. Dakotas could carry around twenty-five

A local boy offers cool drinks to the crew of a BOAC Lodestar that had landed at Juba on the Nile en route for Nairobi.

IWM CH 14077

VIC AVILA

46

passengers. They sat on benches facing each other across the cabin and were very uncomfortable! We could fly those Dakotas for twelve hours because they'd been fitted with extra fuel tanks. Because I was trained on them I was able to sit a number of exams that meant I qualified for a commercial pilot's licence – mind you, back in England I sat all those exams again to get my UK commercial licence, not knowing all I needed to pass was aviation law!'

After another training course on Liberators at Donval, Montreal, Vic had expected to fly to the UK. Instead, after the course it was all change and he found himself on a boat back to England. After two weeks' home leave he was then posted to the Middle East.

'Part of this journey I recall was in an old York which was the civilian version of the Lancaster bomber. We eventually got to Tripoli where on my first night – we were sleeping in tents – I spotted a scorpion in my tent. I hit it with my shoe and despite all the time I spent in the desert that was the only time I saw one of those deadly creatures.

'From then on I spent my time flying passengers to and from India and the Gulf and along the coast of North Africa, Italy and the Balkans, and moving aircraft wherever and whenever they needed to be moved. One interesting plane I flew was a Martin Marauder – a bomber with a tricycle undercarriage – it had two Pratt and Whitney Double Wasp engines and Curtis electric propellers.'

Towards the end of the war Vic was posted to 267 Squadron and followed the front as it moved up through Italy. 'We flew passengers, troops, blood, landmines, rockets, even flea powder!'

Christmas 1944 brought more changes. Vic began flying VIPs around – and other senior military men.

'I think they thought I was a safe pair of hands, but the flying could be nasty – as we flew into Athens airport, for example, we regularly had to jink and fly low over the sea to avoid the machine-gun fire from buildings near the runway and Mount Hymitos. After my time in the VIP unit I was moved to

Malta from where I flew Expediters until the end of the war. I did have one near disaster during the war — it was in June 1945. I was flying an Avro Anson towards Tripoli and lost an engine. I was happily flying on one engine, but that too overheated and lost power and I had to come down in the sea. Neither our training nor the aircraft really took account of the high temperatures in that part of the world, which is why flying with an engine out didn't work for long. None of the passengers or other crew was injured, because it was a good controlled landing. A boat was dropped to us by parachute. But as the parachutes didn't release on touchdown they acted as sails dragging the boat away. I swam after it and just about got there, but was so exhausted I couldn't start the engine. I gave up on engine number one and gave the weakest little pull on engine two — and to my utter astonishment it started first time. If it hadn't started I would not have been able to try again. I cut the parachutes free and navigated the boat to my colleagues who were on the dinghy — and then to the coast about 10 miles away — having both engines running.'

Back in England in 1946 Vic was going to be demobbed so he applied to join British European Airways, the nationalized airline that flew Britain's domestic air routes and those to the Continent.

'The truth is that I desperately wanted to keep flying, but the pilots' jobs had been taken, so I had to go back to the tractor factory! At the same time I joined the RAF Volunteer Reserve at Panshanger and kept flying Chipmunks, and helped instruct younger pilots on instrument flying. But this was all at weekends.

'Then as passenger flying began to boom in the early 1950s pilots were suddenly much in demand and I had many offers of flying jobs.' Vic finally joined BEA in 1951, at Northolt on the northwest edge of London. 'I was paid £625 a year, which was £25 more than pilots who did not have Civil Pilot's Aircraft Licence and Instrument Rating qualifications,' he recalls.

'I flew Vickers Vikings now. Always from Northolt and to destinations all over Europe, but mostly Berlin, Madrid, Gibraltar. Northolt had some tarmac by then but there were still wooden duckboards across the muddy areas. Vickers Vikings were larger than, say, the Dakotas, and faster — they had a cruising speed of about 200mph. They carried about thirty-five passengers and it was at this time that I first flew with stewardesses on board. That was a big change, but it was tough for stewardesses then — they had to know a foreign language, be well educated generally and have a first aid qualification or nursing experience! Although passenger flying had grown considerably since the 1930s and 1940s it

ON BUSINESS FLY
BEA

BRITISH EUROPEAN AIRWAYS

was still something pretty much the preserve of the rich or for people whose tickets were paid for by their employers.

'Flying for most people was also still a huge novelty, which meant almost everyone at some time or other asked to come up on the flight deck – I remember too they always looked with a sort of dreadful fascination at the number of dials and controls we had! I used to explain the intricacies of passenger flying to visitors, of whom one was Gracie Fields – she flew from Naples to Heathrow. I also flew the Greek royal family, the German chancellor and the fiery Cypriot Archbishop Makarios, and many others.

'People who fly today – even in first class – would be surprised at the luxury passengers enjoyed in those early days – with just thirty-five passengers it was easy for the steward and stewardess to give them masses of attention. Their seats were enormous by today's standards, there was room to walk about, silver cutlery and linen napkins were provided so you could eat what was really quite a lavish, though traditional, roast lunch or dinner. Of course we never quite reached the heights of elegance Russian planes adopted – they had candelabra in the cabin on some of their passenger services!'

After the Vickers Vikings Vic went on to fly Viscounts – this was in 1953 and with their gas turbine engines they were the fastest planes in the sky. By this time, too, BEA had moved to Heathrow Airport where the grass runways had given way to metal strips laid on grass – 'that may sound highly dangerous,' says Vic, 'but of course planes were much smaller and lighter than they are today and they were perfectly adequate.'

The Vickers Viscount was a four-engined plane and it carried more passengers than the old Viking. 'We were up from thirty-five to just under fifty passengers and this was the point at which first class was introduced. Before, everyone had travelled one class which was to all intents and purposes first class anyway.

'The Vickers Viscount was totally different from a pilot's point of view from anything that had gone before. Handling was different, even the noise and feel of the engines was different. When you started the Viking engine there was a lot of vibration. On the Viscount it was more like a smooth droning noise with no vibration at all. We used to stand a coin on edge and it would not fall over – you couldn't do that on the Viking or any other early passenger plane I'd flown.

'In terms of speed the gas turbine was a big improvement too – we were up to 300mph now. Even the Americans couldn't compete with the Viscounts. They used to carry spare engines on their DC4s because they always pushed their engines too hard and they frequently broke down! They just couldn't match our schedules and they hated it. We used to hear them complaining over the radio on their company frequency about the problems!

'The other big change from the passengers' point of view was that the Vikings and other earlier planes didn't have pressurized cabins and the Viscount did. Flying higher and faster meant better and more comfortable travel' – as Vic found out while training in the RAF. 'Over Alaska I was once forced to climb to 23,000 feet to avoid weather without a pressurized cabin and without oxygen. I remember getting up and walking over to talk to my navigator and within seconds I was exhausted. I began to move slowly and with the greatest difficulty. I found myself taking very deep breaths due to the lack of oxygen, but being a non-smoker recovered quickly. It's a fact that under these conditions you could get so confused that you'd end up flying in the wrong direction.

'Before pressurization 10,000 feet was the maximum height for passenger planes if you wanted your passengers to be comfortable, but of course people only found this out when they were first able to fly much higher than that. Before, no one had considered that flying high might have these special problems. The other thing about flying really high is that it is very cold so you need heat and air conditioning.

'It was interesting flying to Moscow because we almost always stayed a day or two and in every corridor of the hotel there would be someone stationed to keep an eye on us, clocking you in and out of your room! In Warsaw it was the same.'

VIC AVILA

From Viscounts Vic went on to fly Comet 4bs, the first jet airliner. 'It was a totally different experience – far more powerful. The Comet's controls were power assisted, which made the handling of the plane smooth and easy, but that presented its own problems – as with all high-speed aircraft. If you moved the controls too quickly at high speed you might easily cause damage. To compensate for this artificial control loading was built into the system. Even with the Comet there was a lot to do, however, compared to a modern plane where you have a smaller crew and more automatics – but the workload remains high and everything requires close monitoring. Most stressful times are said to be taking off or coming in to land in adverse weather conditions.'

The first Comets turned out to be liable to stress fractures of the fuselage and several crashed, so when the Comet Mk 4 was finally made available, says Vic, 'it was built like a tank. It would cruise at 550mph which was a big improvement on those old Viscounts.

Incomparable travel comfort

. . . at more than 500 m.p.h.

No aircraft challenges the Comet's combination of jet speed and jet smoothness with world-wide operational suitability.

The Intercontinental Comet carries about 55 to 80 passengers on 3,000-mile stages at more than 500 m.p.h.
The continental Comet carries about 80 to 100 passengers on short inter-city stages at up to 545 m.p.h.
Neither is dependent upon dense and continually growing traffic, or upon enlarged airports.

COMET
(ROLLS-ROYCE AVON R.A. 29 ENGINES)

DE HAVILLAND WORLD ENTERPRISE

'The Viscounts carried forty-seven passengers when they first came in and about seventy-one at the finish – the Comet carried about 120. I was always being trained as new aircraft came in and by the late 1960s I was on BAC 1-11 500 Series and Trident IIIs. The Tridents were the fastest of the passenger jets and it was said that they only got airborne on take-off due to the curvature of the earth!

'By the time I retired in December 1977, piston-engined aircraft for commercial passenger flying seemed just a distant memory.'

PLAYER'S CIGARETTES

DRYAD

IMPERIAL AIRWAYS LINER "DRYAD" : "DIANA" CLASS

THE WORST BUMPS
IN THE AIR

Our departure from Stag Lane Aerodrome was of great interest and no little amusement to those who saw us off. Stowing the spares, luggage and equipment on board seemed to be the chief business of the day. Firstly we carried underneath the cabin a spare propeller, which had been carefully covered in canvas and screened off. Then there was a certain number of small spare parts that might be required for the machine and engine. Emmott seemed to have a terrific amount of camera gear to pack away, for, apart from the cinematograph camera, there were many thousands of feet of film to be carried and a hefty ungainly tripod. Then there was my own little cine-camera and still camera, Emmott's press camera, and I believe Elliott had one also. Then again we had guns to go on board, because I came to the conclusion that, should we by any misfortune have to land in some uninhabited country or tractless jungle, the guns would not only be a protection but might be our only means of getting food after we had exhausted our few days' emergency rations.

On the following day we flew on to Lyons in indifferent weather, and as the hour was too late for us to make Pisa, our intended next stop, we pushed on to Marseille instead and there spent the night. Bad weather welcomed us next morning, but after it had cleared a little we flew on again for Pisa.

This flight gave me an opportunity to prove what I have said so many times, that the worst bumps in the air are not experienced necessarily in the heat of the tropics, or from hot or cold air rising, but through up and down currents caused by gales dashing over mountains. As a rule the Riviera coastline is one of the great fine weather spots of the world, and the view from an aeroplane flying at a few thousand feet, 2 or 3 miles out to sea, is a sight that will never be forgotten by anyone who is fortunate enough to witness it.

As one looks northwards towards the land, there is a deep blue sea in the foreground below such as is not known round the British Isles, and its silver crested breakers dash in a mass of white foam on a rocky shore. From an altitude of 3000 or 4000 feet Monte Carlo looks like a collection of fairy palaces clustered on the cliff side, with a little model harbour where perhaps one or two trim steam yachts lie at anchor, and beyond the breakwater, contrasting so vividly with the blue ocean, the snow-white sails of various skiffs.

As one's eye travels beyond the town, there appears a view of massive precipitous cliffs, cut with mountain road-ways that are really fine engineering feats. High up on these mountain slopes can be seen ancient little villages, very often built on pinnacles, belonging to a bygone age when the native of this coastline had to take refuge in his own small stronghold from the barbarian who might invade him from Northern Europe, or from the pirate and adventurer of the sea. Higher still are fresh mountain ranges with deep valleys, and beyond are the snow-capped Alps whose vividness is intensified by the brilliant sunshine, so that the cloudless blue sky against which these peaks are silhouetted seems to merge into a turquoise hue on the horizon.

When we flew along this coastline one day last November, a vastly different spectacle was to be seen. The sky was overcast and grey, while the Alps were buried in low cloud and mist; but the weather condition which caused us real trouble was the violent, strong north-east wind which for hundreds of miles was dashing over these ice-clad peaks. The result was that by the time the gale had reached the Mediterranean the whole atmosphere seemed to be carried in one mighty chopped-up downrush to the sea.

The further we proceeded along the coastline the more violent became the atmosphere, and so I thought that by flying low under the cliff we might possibly avoid the main disturbance; but here the down current was so violent that it was difficult to keep the machine on an even keel. I then decided to climb to a high altitude in search of a calmer zone so, opening out the engine and pulling back the control lever, we very quickly shot up to 6,000 feet. But the higher we went the worse became the bumps, and the machine at times seemed to be almost uncontrollable.

Emmott and Elliott in the cabin were having a very rough time, for it was with great difficulty that they could keep in their seats. While Elliott strove to keep the baggage in position, Emmott was struggling with his beloved camera which I thought might be broken at any moment, as very often baggage and passengers' heads touched the roof of the cabin as the machine was caught in some violent down current.

All this took place in a very short space of time, and we quickly decided that the only course of action was to get away from the trouble, the mountains; and so we headed for the open sea. This was not sufficient to get rid of all the bumps, and I resorted to an old plan that I had practised so often before; we flew right out to sea, away from the shore and very low over the water which evidently acts as a cushion for the down currents of the wind, and gives a more or less steady, even atmosphere. In this way we continued across the bay before Genoa, skimming over the sea within 20 feet of the water, in fact so low were we flying that when we encountered a fleet of fishing smacks it was necessary to climb a little to clear their masts. It was here we had the little thrill of flashing by these boats as they were tossed in the rough sea, much to the excitement of the fishermen who waved vigorously to us as we flew on our way.

Alan Cobham,
one of the great
aviation pioneers.

At last Pisa was reached, and as the day was too short for us to reach our next destination before dark, we decided to stay the night, and if possible see the leaning tower before dusk.

On the following day we had a comparatively simple flight over almost the whole length of Italy to our next landing place, Grottaglie near Taranto at the heel of Italy. Here we were most enthusiastically received by the Italian Commandant who greeted us the moment we landed, while in his trail followed one of the mess stewards, carrying a tray of bottles and glasses with all the requirements necessary for any cocktail that one might mention.

My Flight to the Cape and Back, Alan Cobham, 1926

TED WILLIAMS
NAVIGATOR

The navigational systems on modern jet aeroplanes are staggeringly precise and complex. Radar and global satellite positioning systems mean that any and every movement can be precisely calculated and the exact whereabouts of an aircraft are always known. But it wasn't always like this. In the early days of passenger flying the skill of the navigator was vital to keep an aeroplane on track – and in many instances the navigator would be using methods almost identical to those used by Elizabethan mariners!

Ted Williams is one of the fast dwindling generation of early air navigators. Tall, thin and immensely polite, he still wears the crisp military moustache that bears witness to his early days in the Air Force.

Ted joined up straight from school in 1942 aged just eighteen. And it was his Air Force training that was later to lead to a secondment to British Overseas Airways Corporation – BOAC – and operating the early passenger services that crisscrossed the world. But Ted's initial decision to apply to the Air Force rather than the Army or Navy can be attributed, as he admits himself, to the glamour and excitement of flying – flying seemed easily the most romantic of all the options, but, as he explains, 'Everyone knew they would be called up, but I thought I'd apply anyway. And of course it wasn't just a question of joining the Air Force and saying, "Oh, I want to be a pilot" or whatever. They did the selecting. If you passed the interview, as I did, you were sent to what was called the Air Crew Reception Centre in London. We spent several weeks

PLAYER'S CIGARETTES

IMPERIAL AIRWAYS LINER "ENSIGN"

there being sorted out into different roles. We never knew exactly – and I still don't to this day – how they decided whether one was to be a pilot, a bombardier or a navigator but we were all to be aircrew, that much we did know.

'The real selection was I suspect more to do with numbers than anything else. Anyway after the interview and some flying it was decided that I was to become what was known then as an observer – that name for a navigator went right back to the dawn of military flying in the Great War when the Air Force was still the Royal Flying Corps. In those very early aircraft of course the observer merely sat in the back seat – or the front seat – map reading and lobbing out an occasional bomb. By 1942 navigation was a bit more complex but the old name was retained until well into the war.'

After selection Ted and his fellow would-be navigators were sent for training. Few were trained in England – the British dominions, particularly Canada and South Africa, were usually chosen as training grounds instead because they were well away from the main theatres of hostilities. But for the new recruits going abroad was all part of the adventure.

'I'd never been abroad before when I set sail for Canada on the *Queen Mary*. We actually went first to New York and then caught a train to a place called Portage La Prairie in Manitoba. Here the training was pretty intensive but enjoyable. I remember the wonderful weather – endless blue skies – and of course it was those almost guaranteed clear conditions that made Canada such a good place to train pilots, bomb aimers, and navigators.

'Our nine months' training consisted of quite a number of things that are actually common to all aircrew – safety procedures, for example, like how to put on a parachute, but as a navigator I also had far more esoteric things to learn. I have no certainties about this but I have a suspicion that I might well have been selected as a navigator because at my initial interview I had talked about my mathematical abilities. I was good at spherical trigonometry and I suspect they rather liked that!

'After a while we got down to the really serious business of navigating. I had to learn how to read maps and charts, plot a course, find my position using the stars.

'Using the stars to navigate was indeed very much what a medieval or Elizabethan mariner would have done, and although it might sound absurd to try to use a slow method like this on a rapidly moving thing like an aeroplane you have to remember that those we flew in then might be travelling at a maximum ground speed against a head wind of about 96mph. By today's

TED WILLIAMS

56

standards that's almost a walking pace! So there was actually plenty of time to use the stars to work out the position of the aeroplane.

'Using the stars like this was essential even on what might sound like a straightforward simple journey. Take crossing the Mediterranean from Gibraltar to Cairo, for example – even this journey involved checking the stars because radio beacons on the ground were few and far between.

'The on-board equipment for the navigator included what was known as the astrodome – a perspex hemisphere above your head that was optically calibrated. This meant you could see the stars and measure their positions accurately.'

A BOAC navigator takes a reading on the sun half way through a transatlantic flight.
IWM CH 15449

Ted trained on an Avro Anson, a twin-engined monoplane that was just big enough to carry two pupils, a pilot and wireless operator. Back in the UK he was to fly in Wellingtons – twin-engined bombers that were far bigger than the Anson but with virtually no extra room, largely because all the space had been designed to take a maximum bomb load.

After nine months' training in Canada he returned to the UK for three months' operational training at Bramcote in the Midlands, near Leicester.

'This was far more specific training because by now I had my badge as a fully paid-up navigator. I was as rich as Croesus! An aircraftman under training was paid three shillings and sixpence a day but at the end of training that went up to twelve shillings and sixpence a day – a huge boost! I've never had so much money in my life!

'After training in the UK my colleagues who immediately began to go on bombing missions suffered dreadful casualties – I think I'm right in saying that 20 per cent of them were killed. And this was not always the result of enemy action – quite a few were killed in accidents caused by inexperience. These were crashes that simply shouldn't have happened, but we were getting towards the end of the war and youngsters were being trained very quickly, perhaps too quickly. It's certainly true to say that if you survived the first few months in the air your chances of surviving the war increased dramatically.'

While most of his colleagues went off on bombing missions in Europe or the Far East, Ted was seconded to BOAC, which had recently been created out of the old Imperial Airways. It was 1944 and he went down to BOAC headquarters in Bristol where he spent a few weeks before being sent to Poole in Dorset.

'Each of the new arrivals did two trips from Bristol to Lisbon on DC3 Dakotas – I think I'm right in saying that was the most popular aircraft ever built. The other main reason we were sent to Bristol was to have our uniforms made – that uniform with its gold braid stayed pretty much unchanged right through until well into the British Airways period.

'As soon as I got to the Poole base a man walked up to me and without a word of introduction said, "Right, come and have a look at one of our boats – I want you in India by Friday!" Taking up the medieval mariner theme again I should point out that in those days we called our flights voyages and we always had to fill out a voyage report when we got back. I had no experience of flying boats until that first trip but I went as a second navigating officer with a chap who knew them inside out. We were doing the job from the outset but of course we continually took advice.

A Short Sunderland lands at Bathurst in The Gambia, West Africa in 1945.

IWM CH 15442

'I remember on that first voyage – we flew a Short Sunderland – we had two pilots, a fully experienced navigator (in addition to me), an engineer and a radio officer. The Short Sunderland had a sort of turret for the navigator to see the stars – it was eventually taken off on later models. But those early flying boats were very different in many respects from later models. For example they had only rough metal benches for the passengers to sit on.

'By the time of the Hythe Class flying boat things were far more comfortable – in fact the Hythe had a long career, continuing I think until 1957.'

Ted's first flight to India was far more straightforward than he'd expected. He flew first to Gibraltar, then Cairo, then on to Basra, Karachi and finally Calcutta. As the Japanese were still in control of much of the Far East the flying boats could go no further, and voyages to Australia were not resumed until 1946. But Ted enjoyed his new role immensely despite the long hours in the air. 'It took two weeks to fly to India but that wasn't always what we did – often we would work a shuttle back and forth between Calcutta and Karachi. We were sometimes on a shuttle like that for as long as six weeks at a time, and the rate at which we flew shuttles and long voyages generally increased after the Japanese surrendered. We were often flying British prisoners of war back to England at this stage. We also flew hours that would terrify today's regulators. You might easily do sixteen hours at a stretch but I think it was less dangerous than it may sound because the pace of flying was relatively leisurely. We were still only up to speeds of, say, 100–125mph, so the navigator could get his positions sorted, and his headings, and then stop for lunch.

'In the same way the captain and first officer had a relatively leisurely time – the captain took time off when the first officer took over and the first officer took time off for a snooze when I relieved him. Of course all this applied only if the weather was good – everything changed if we had bad weather or some other difficulty.

'The tool of the navigator's trade was the bubble sextant – instead of a bar positioned on the horizon (as sailors have in their sextants) we used a bubble to give us our level position. It wasn't always easy to use – if the aeroplane accelerated, for example, the bubble would move and give you the wrong level. We got round this problem by taking readings over two minutes to get a reasonable average. Later models of the Mk 9 Bubble Sextant had a clockwork drive that helped you keep your star aligned with the bubble while you set a clock going to record two minutes' worth of sights. Once or twice things did go wrong, I recall, and we did drift off course. This might happen if – without wanting to get too technical – you crossed what we called the centre of a pressure system. This meant the isobars were in the wrong direction and you might drift as much as, say, 20 degrees to starboard or whatever. However, we always picked up the error pretty quickly.

'Another difficulty we experienced was with air traffic controllers at Karachi: they would never contradict us if we were wrong when we gave our position – they always simply assumed we must be right, which is a very dangerous thing for an air traffic controller to do. If you asked for a bearing they would simply try to give you the bearing they thought you thought you were on, if that makes sense! Perhaps it was simply the habit of deference to the British! But anyway, you needed nerves of steel to fly into Karachi when they were in the mood to agree with everything!

'The thing you have to remember about navigating by the stars is that it enabled the flying boats to travel at night – without star navigation that would have been far more difficult. In those days we described a journey or voyage as "being sent down the route", but the routes changed as the war developed and changed again after it ended. But even when the war was raging the Poole to Cairo part of the voyage was really the only section dramatically affected by the fighting. To reduce the risk of attack we would fly south and west from Poole down across the Atlantic and then turn east for Gibraltar – that broad sweeping detour enabled us to avoid the Germans.

'Other difficulties for the navigators were, for example, crossing the Arabian Desert, which we did from time to time. Here, of course, the sands were as empty of landmarks as the most empty ocean, so it was difficult to fly across during the day when there were no stars to help fix your position. The

solution was to use the sun or a radio signal to give you your latitude and then elapsed time to give you longitude, or a radio bearing which you would cross with your latitude reading taken from the sun. Sometimes when the moon was visible during daylight you could use that.

'Later on, towards the end of my time in civil aviation, a wonderful navigational device came in. The Constellation was fitted with a radar altimeter. This compared a height given by radio altimeter with a reading from a barometric altimeter. Without getting too much into the technicalities, this meant you were measuring the pressure difference. A periodic reading would establish whether you were going into high or low pressure and therefore the drift to right or left. We called it Pressure Pattern Flying.

'Another technique we used was called Single Heading Flight. For this you measured the barometric pressure at your departure point and at your destination. Given those two pieces of information you could then work out what your heading should be to get from the one place to the other.

'I didn't get far with that technique because air traffic control began to come in and establish lanes for air traffic. Before that there were no lanes or corridors. I first came across air lanes in the USA where they had them by 1946 or 1947. They first came in for the UK on Atlantic routes, and then gradually they spread to all other routes from the UK and made all our wonderful navigation methods redundant.'

As navigation techniques improved so too did those early flying boats, with the ex-military Sunderlands being developed into the more luxurious Hythes. Then in 1947 Ted left flying boats and moved on to Constellations, the graceful four-engined American airliners, a few examples of which still sometimes visit British air shows. He worked on Constellations for eighteen months before transferring back into the Air Force where his career was to take him in a very different direction.

'I thought that I could be going back and forth over the Atlantic for ever or go back to the Air Force for a wider career. So in 1949 that's what I did. As I'd been in transport, as it were, the military authorities sent me to Transport Command. Very soon afterwards I was posted to the Central Navigation School where I instructed staff navigators.

'But to go back to those early passenger aircraft – it was an extraordinary time. Although we carried the odd freight package those flying boats were in fact the very first real attempt to create civilian passenger flying as a normal everyday activity. Of course, having said that, it has to be remembered that only a tiny number of people ever flew with us — and they were almost all diplomats, or Senior Service officers. We estimated that it cost two and a half times what BOAC was actually earning to carry each passenger.

'A good example of how different it all was can be judged by the time we took Field Marshall Wavell — who had been commander of British troops in North Africa — to his new post as Viceroy in India. We asked him if he would like us to bend our route over North Africa so he could look out once more at Tobruk! He was fascinated.

'I remember we also regularly flew ENSA artists to India or Cairo. By this stage the cabin on the Hythe had been completely redesigned from the days of rough old steel benches — in fact it was now more comfortable than today's first class. The seating pattern was more like it often is in a first-class railway carriage, with a pair of seats facing each other across a table. And we only carried a maximum of twenty-two passengers.

'The one problem for aircrew that you certainly don't get now is that the noise of the engines tended to cause high tone deafness — in other words you could lose the ability to hear high notes.

'I suppose it was quite a glamorous life because we did get the chance to stay in Cairo or Basra or wherever while we waited for our next aircraft. You'd slip — or change — crews, but not on every leg of a journey. You might slip for a week — and this could be very pleasant. In Cairo, for example, BOAC had a luxurious Nile cruiser for crew accommodation.

BOAC houseboat at Leopoldville. IWM CH15314

SHORTEST DISTANCE
BETWEEN 2 POINTS

NEW SPEED TO SHORTEN THE DISTANCE

<u>QUIET</u> LUXURY TO MAKE THE TIME FLY

Largest, Roomiest Airliner in the World
Far Quieter for Greater Comfort • Wider Aisles
Larger Windows • Wider Seats
Finest Air Conditioning • Restful 5-Cabin Privacy
Congenial Starlight Lounge
Interior Design by Henry Dreyfuss
The Fastest Constellation Ever Built.

For all the speed, and quiet comfort, too,
fly Super Constellations over every ocean and
continent on these 19 leading airlines:

AIR FRANCE • AIR-INDIA INTERNATIONAL • AVIANCA
CUBANA • DEUTSCHE LUFTHANSA • EASTERN AIR LINES
IBERIA • KLM • LAV • NORTHWEST ORIENT AIRLINES
PAKISTAN INTERNATIONAL • QANTAS • SEABOARD & WESTERN
SLICK AIRWAYS • TAP • THAI AIRWAYS
TRANS-CANADA AIR LINES • TWA-TRANS WORLD AIRLINES • VARIG

LOCKHEED SUPER CONSTELLATION

Look to Lockheed for Leadership

'I'm not absolutely sure but I think all the captains I flew with are now dead, but that's not really surprising when you think that most of them had a World War I background in the Royal Flying Corps. Their experience went right back to the very beginning of flying – they'd flown primitive World War I planes. The Hythes and Sunderlands would have seemed incredibly sophisticated by comparison. Radio officers tended to be even older, but of course there were exceptions and I met several radio officers who'd come in the way I had and were my sort of age.

'It's easy to think that passenger flying covered only a very limited number of routes in those pre-jet days but in fact BOAC alone flew many routes, including from Scotland to Sweden. They also had a North Atlantic route between Baltimore and Poole which was flown with Boeing 314s, a large four-engined flying boat. Conditions on this for the crew were luxurious – the chart table for the navigator, for example, seemed as big a skating rink!

'Before stewards became a part of flying the flight engineer would bring the flasks of hot food on board and we all just helped ourselves. I always had my lunch at the chart table and it always seemed to be stew of some kind.

'In the early days there were no seat belts for crew or passengers – I think I'm right in saying they first started to be used on the North Atlantic routes because the turbulence was always worst there.'

By 1949 Ted was back in the Air Force. Three years later his career took an unusual turn when he was sent off to learn Russian. The plan was that having learned the language he would expect to be either employed to monitor Russian broadcasts or be sent to Moscow as an attaché. After several years working seven days a week till 10 p.m. he passed the Interpreter's Examination. Then he went into the monitoring business and, as he says, 'Life was never the same again for me,' although he did not yet leave the flying world entirely. He went to the Aeroplane and Armament Experimental Establishment, Boscombe Down, to help test Vulcans and Victors, the RAF's V-bombers, built to carry Britain's nuclear missiles. They were frighteningly sophisticated, he says, but despite their high-tech navigation systems he always kept his sextant for emergencies! Eventually Ted went to Russia for two stints – first as an assistant air attaché in 1964 and then finally as the UK's Defence Attaché in 1972 before retiring as an air commander in 1982.

'I still meet a gang of Russian speakers every now and then and I've never forgotten those early navigational skills. It's sad that they are no longer of any value, but at least they helped keep those early aircraft safe in the air.'

THE PLANE-CALLER

The aeroplane propellers were rolling the drums. Rolling the drums at the airport in Miami! The motor throats of the Pan American fleet of flying boats were open and bellowing down the airways of the world.

Sunshine and flowers, and over all the motor-drums. Blue sky and laughter, and the music of the motors on the air. Cosmopolitan aeroplane luggage, chic travelling clothes, a smart dining room done modern, with silver wings on the walls, and the biggest 'floor show' ever put on by any restaurant in the world – the Pan American planes taking off across the restaurant windows while the diners watched! And above the bursts of laughter, over the cool tinkle of ice against glass, over all the musical accompaniment of china on silver, the voice of the plane-caller calling the planes.

'Havana! Havana plane!'

Broadcasting over the airport, over the hum of the propellers, over the hangars and the waiting rooms.

'Plane for Ha—va—na – leaving on P—i—e—r – Six. All passengers please present tickets for Havana – immediately – on Pier Six.'

Thunders and cannonades and crashes! Roars and waves of sound! Drumming up the armies of the air!

Big, four-motored Brazilian clipper ship taking off. Rolling the drums! Exciting – delighting – premonitory! The music of the spheres – the Valkyrie cry – the air call – the call of the blood to the ears that heed the rumble of the airport drums!

A new race of men mingled among the gay, carefree, transient throngs of the airport – a race of men who walked under the silver wings on the walls, and wore golden wings across their hearts. These were the aeroplane pilots. They had a certain striking, almost family resemblance to one another, so that even without the golden wings they would be marked out by the observant anywhere in the world as airmen.

'Do you mean that tall, blond airplane pilot?' Claudia heard the lady at the next table ask her husband.

'They're all tall and blond,' her husband laughed. 'Almost all. When you've been flying for a while you'll recognize the joke of trying to identify one of these boys by calling him a tall, blond aviator.'

'But why should they all look alike?' the lady insisted.

'Who knows?' her husband said. 'The type of the adventurous, perhaps?'

'Do you suppose,' Claudia asked her Aunt Naomi, who was having breakfast with her, 'do you suppose if I should fly long enough I shall be tall and blonde?'

'I'm afraid not,' her aunt laughed, looking discouragingly at Claudia's five-foot, entirely too round, hopelessly brunette, extremely unadventurous figure.

'Key West – Key West! All passengers for Key West!'

'Puerto Rico! All passengers on P–i–e–r Ten – for Puerto Rico!'

'Kingston – Kingston, Jamaica! All passengers——"

'Port au Prince – Port au Prince – Haiti! All passengers – for Port au Prince – on P–i–e–r——five!"

Claudia's heart skipped a beat. For she was going to Port au Prince! Her new black alligator shoes started taking her as fast as they could to Pier 5. But her courage was lagging behind. This was her first flight over the ocean. And she was scared!

Until this minute the great Pan American Airways cruise around South America which had been planned for her had seemed a magical story in a book. But this Pier 5 stuff was concrete.

A last glance up, while she was still free to see how much air there really is between sea and sky. How far, how far, how far to fall! And all the time her new shoes were going right on to Pier 5 – on out to the open float, beside which the Commodore for Port au Prince sat so soigné and smart upon the blue water, with a bright red band round its breast and silver wings.

The tall, blond captain of the Commodore stood on the dock beside his ship. Very important and reassuring-looking. In fact, the tall, blond captain in blue was the only thing of any importance whatever in the entire world to Claudia. Nor was she the only passenger to regard him thus. The new, young college graduate from Washington tried to get the captain to guarantee good weather all the way. The 'hard-boiled' businessman shook hands and said, 'Well, Captain, I'm leaving myself in your hands.' And the lady passenger first in line approached determinedly.

'Captain Extrom,' she asked firmly, 'what time shall we get to Port au Prince?'

'We could get there by four o'clock this afternoon,' Captain Extrom said, 'if we could only keep this tailwind we've got now.'

'Then why can't we keep it?' the lady demanded indignantly. 'Why don't they put tailwinds on all these planes?'

Everybody looked up and grinned at the captain as the passengers went up over the rounded, shiny side of the silver ship on polite, steady rubber-covered steps, and down a cute little silver stairway into the silver inside.

'Oh, my soul!' Claudia gasped to herself. 'It looks like that submarine I

went down in at Pearl Harbor, in Honolulu. I'd better get out.'

She was being pushed along an aisle, and saw her bright new coat folded neatly on a seat beside a window. That was a help. She sank into the luxuriously upholstered chair on top of the coat. In the seat facing her was the lady passenger who had demanded that tailwinds be put on all planes. And the lady had a copy of a new magazine in her hand.

And such is life that with the sight of the new coat and the cheery magazine cover Claudia settled back in the flying boat and was suddenly, immediately, and for all time airminded.

From the small, square window she watched her Aunt Naomi waving goodbye. While she was wondering how deep the Caribbean Sea was really supposed to be – just in case the flying boat fell into it – she noted that there was a rose-coloured velvet carpet on the floor, and tiny velvet curtains at the windows. And that was a help too. For such is feminine psychology that it can face any unknown – provided it is on a rose-coloured carpet!

The speed of the motors increased. The silver ship shivered. Claudia put her hand flat against the arched steel ceiling to assure herself that it was solid, and – it wasn't solid at all! It shook like a leaf.

'Oh, my soul! It is a leaf! In the wind!' She shuddered. 'Less than a leaf – less than a leaf! And maybe I'd better get out!'

But the boat was moving. Or else the sky was sliding. Snow-white spray dashed in uncountable sparkling needlepoints against the window panes. The boat skimmed over the water, beating up meringue all round it. Faster, faster – to the drum of the motors, singing the song of all the past of men upon the earth – of all the promise of men upon the moon! A final quadruple roar! A wall of water, solid, opaque against the windows, shutting out everything!

'I guess we're sinking now,' she shouted at the lady with the new magazine. 'And I've never seen South America!'

Then everything suddenly emerged into sunshine. The cute little twin

lozenge-shaped silver pontoons under the wings of the
ship sloped up, dripping like bird's feet tucked up under
its breast. Crystal necklaces of water shone in the sun
and roped and rolled off the shiny sides of the gallant,
gay little pontoons. Below was blue water, and above was blue sky.

And in between was Claudia – alone. Forgetting in flight all save flight
itself. Forgetting all save that the race to which she belonged, and she with it,
had conquered another element. That deep in the hidden dimension of her
own consciousness was unfolding the crumpled leaf of evolution to the air,
while something in her soul exulted, 'My God, I've got wings!'

Steady as a strong breeze sailed the elegant, chic, cosmopolitan
Commodore. Skimming for enchanted, unblemished, opalescent hours 500
feet above the thin blue water of the Caribbean Sea. On the purple pools the
salmon-coloured shadows fell, and over the emerald isles and above the
turquoise-blue bays and the cool-bathed coral-beds. All lay below upon the
Caribbean like the jewels of a Titan empress strewn in gorgeous carelessness
across the mirrors of her dressing table.

'Oh, I can't stand it! It's too much beauty! Too, too much!' Claudia
babbled mentally, incoherently, to herself.

'"If I had the wings of an angel,"' her mind kept on hypnotically repeating
to the music of the motors.

> 'If I had the wings of an angel,
> Over these prison walls would I fly,
> Straight to the arms of my darling,
> And there I'd be willing to die!

'Oh, I can't stand it, because it's too beautiful!'
Looking over the side, she made her first acquaintance with the friendly
little airship shadow that accompanied the ship. As she watched it she made it
a foolish little song under her breath:

> 'The airship had a little shadow;
> Its shape was on the sea;
> And everywhere the airship went
> The shadow was sure to be.'

Afterwards, for many, many days, over many, many seas and many foreign
shores, she was never alone, for she had the little shadow. Odd, comforting
little thoughts the air breeds in the human mind; she always called the little
shadow 'we'.

Sky Gipsy, Claudia Cranston, 1936

OLIVE CARLISLE
STEWARDESS

In a relatively short career as an air stewardess with BOAC during the late 1940s and early 1950s, Olive Carlisle managed to achieve several notable firsts. She was among the first batch of stewardesses ever taken on by BOAC, for example, and then became the first stewardess to work on a British flying boat.

Like many young women who grew up in the years after the end of the Great War, Olive, who was born in 1921, refused to accept many of the restrictions on what women could do that her parents and grandparents would have taken for granted.

She grew up in a village near Diss in Norfolk, and while at school decided she would go to college and then get a job, rather than relying on a suitable husband turning up and providing her with a role at home. But by the time she was in her late teens another war seemed inevitable and she decided to join up. The Women's Auxiliary Air Force turned her down flat simply because she was too young, so at seventeen she left school and joined the Civil Service, where she worked in the valuation office department helping estimate the costs of families whose homes had been destroyed by bombing. She stayed in the Civil Service for two years – until 1941 – and then tried once more to join up.

A slight but very animated figure who looks far younger than she is, Olive still chuckles at the recollection of her determination.

'Well, we all wanted to do our bit, we were very single-minded – the sense of patriotism we had then is difficult to understand now, but everyone felt it.'

PLAYER'S CIGARETTES

IMPERIAL AIRWAYS FLYING-BOAT "SATYRUS"

OLIVE CARLISLE

72

Olive was then told that her job was a reserved occupation. She refused to accept this, offered her resignation and became what was officially known as a rebel volunteer.

'Eventually my boss had to let me go, otherwise I suppose he might have been seen as someone who was trying to stop us heroes going into action,' she says with a smile. 'Mind you, I knew my job would be kept open for me when I got back from the war, but I never fancied it much and when I did go back just to look round after the war ended I found all the papers I'd left years earlier were in just the same positions and covered in dust. It seemed to sum up the nature of the job.'

Finally accepted by the WAAF as a Volunteer Reserve, she went into the radar section. This was enormously exciting as radar then was incredibly secret.

'Oh, it was very hush-hush. You couldn't mention the fact that you were involved with it or had the faintest idea how it worked to anyone. Wives even had to keep it secret from their husbands and vice versa; there were very few married WAAFs.'

Radar training was thorough but speedy, and a few months after joining up Olive found herself being sent from one tracking station to the next.

'I was sent to radar stations all over the country, but the job was pretty much always the same – in simple terms we saw, and gave warning of, the approach of every aircraft by watching a blip on a screen.'

Anyone who's seen a war film will be completely familiar with the basic radar set-up, but during the war it was positively space age, as Olive explains.

'We couldn't talk to the aircraft – that was still some years away – but radar was considered to be an astonishing innovation. We could pick up an aircraft's signal and plot its course. It took me about a month to learn how to operate the radar and later on I spent a year instructing others on it. Then, after training for a commission as Signals/Radar Officer, I learned Morse and was stationed at RAF Dunkirk near Canterbury for a while in charge of teleprinters and wireless operations and mechanics.'

Throughout this time Olive hoped she would be posted abroad. Like many servicemen and women, she felt that the real action was on the Continent and she wanted to be in the thick of it.

'Yes, it was partly that and partly that I desperately wanted to travel. By the time I got my chance the war was in its last stages. I was sent to 72 Wing HQ Mons and then on to Bonn. Radar operators followed the front up as the Germans retreated. We had mobile stations and the idea was that we used our radar to guide our bombers and then sent them a signal when they were in position above their target – it meant they could fly through or above cloud and still bomb accurately through it. Eventually my job became one of testing the operators to make sure they got official qualifications for their work.'

When Olive was first posted abroad she was the only girl in a mess with about one hundred men, which led to one or two slightly odd routines.

'They used to play "Goodnight Ladies" on the piano in the mess after dinner when they knew it was all going to get a bit raucous, and I knew it was time to make a discreet retreat!'

When the war ended Olive's taste for travel and adventure was stronger than ever, but the competition for jobs was going to be fierce as tens of thousands of men were also returning from the front.

'When I was demobbed at the end of 1945 I still had itchy feet, I suppose, so I went to an employment

bureau in London looking for a job involving travel. I had seen an advert for stewardesses and I hoped I might have a chance. Imagine my disappointment then, when the assistant said that it was a pity I hadn't arrived a week earlier because they'd been recruiting air stewardesses for BOAC, but that the recruitment programme had closed the day before I arrived. I felt I'd been so unlucky, but they sent me to see if the situation was any better at British European Airways. They offered me a vacancy, but it was on teleprinters and I'd already tried that and didn't like it at all.

'When I got back to the bureau I heard that an Air Commodore, Vic Marshal, under whom I'd served during the war, had come into the office while I was away, seen my name on a list and recommended me for anything that might be available, which just shows how important luck can be in life. Suddenly I was able to join the potential recruits on the BOAC recruitment programme. I went up before their selection board along with 300 other hopefuls. That 300 had been whittled down from 3000 so I was very lucky. But then I found out that I was even luckier because I was one of just twelve chosen from those 300 interviewees. We were the first stewardesses ever taken on by BOAC who had until then only employed stewards, except for a very short period before the war when women were taken on for the Foynes-USA line.

'We were told we'd been recruited to work on Solent flying boats. After our medicals we were sent to London and then to Aldermaston in Berkshire. The comprehensive course lasted three months, and also covered many eventualities we hoped we'd never experience. We were taught about the sort of food that might be edible if we ever had to make a forced landing on some uninhabited tropical island and how to catch dew at night if we should be forced down in the desert.

'One thing we were taught that we did need to know was what was called silver service – basically the technique for serving food – and we were supposed already to know some first aid, which I did, and at least two foreign languages. I had French and German which I'd learned at school and greatly improved during my time in Bonn and Mons.'

Olive was put through three months of what she describes as hard but excellent training, but then came disappointment.

'We were told that the flying boats weren't ready so we were sent to Imperial House in Buckingham Palace Road, which was BOAC's London Terminal, to practise our waitressing skills in the basement restaurant. We were really being used as cheap labour, but we just had to get on with it.

'I remember this was 1947 and the summer was so hot that girls were fainting from heat in the restaurant, and we had to ask special permission to take our thick uniform jackets off!'

Gradually Olive and her fellow new recruits were taken off these duties – some went to work on BOAC's American routes, some to the East Africa and Middle East line working on Dakotas. And that's where Olive was finally sent.

'Working on Dakotas was fun because we'd at least escaped the restaurant and the planes themselves were not as basic as they'd been in the war. The old bucket seats that had been fitted to the Dakotas during the war years had been taken out and they were fitted with much more comfortable seats. Of course the seats had none of the electric buttons they later had.'

Olive worked very long hours from the outset. On one trip back from

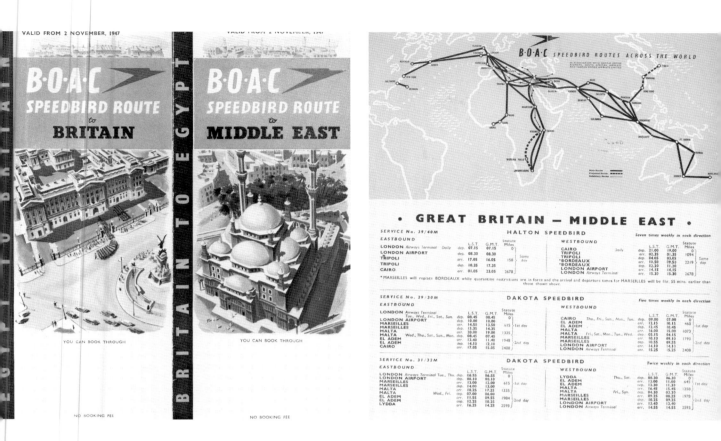

Nairobi to Cairo she remembers working continually for fifteen and a half hours apart from half hour stops at Juba and Malakal without a break, but even working at this pace had its compensations, as she explains.

'At least when we arrived we didn't immediately turn round and go back as they do now. And we didn't fly at night on flying boats so we always had a good night's sleep in a hotel somewhere.'

Despite the improvements described by Olive, the Dakotas were still pretty rough and ready by the standards of today's aeroplanes. They were very bumpy and very noisy – with their unpressurized cabins, 7000 feet was the maximum cruising height except for short periods.

'Flying at that level could be very scary because you couldn't easily get above bad weather. I was afraid on a few occasions but more so were the passengers because most of those who flew with us – particularly those emigrating – had never flown before. Our training was really good and we'd had it drummed into us that we must always seem calm and confident, so we did. On the Dakotas there were no stewards – just us girls. The truth is of course that in those days the passengers were spoiled to bits. We had more

time, there were fewer passengers and we got to know them and their little foibles, their likes and dislikes.'

The stewardess was responsible for checking all her equipment onto the flight and then off again and any failure to do this meticulously could have financial consequences. 'Oh, that was a real nuisance because when I say we had to check everything before take-off I mean everything – cutlery, napkins, glasses, cups, bowls, sugar tongs, blankets, magazines. You name it and it was our responsibility. And if you didn't hand everything back to the stores the cost of the missing items could be deducted from your wages, so we always had to keep an eye out at ground stops, particularly for vanishing blankets or cutlery. We were paid about £6 a week. The details of all our flights had to be entered in our individual logbooks, although pretty soon very few bothered with this and our bosses never said anything.'

Olive worked on Dakotas from October 1947 until the following spring – about six months, but she says that looking back it seems much longer. Dakotas flew from Heathrow, and passengers were assembled in large tents at 'North End' before boarding. Crew also reported for duty at the North End. Olive agrees these were exciting days but somehow they didn't have the glamour of the flying boats.

'Well, in comparison, flying boats were known to be the last word in sophistication and luxury. And it was the spring of 1948 when at last I found myself posted to Southampton.' BOAC had just acquired a fleet of new Short Solent flying boats – the biggest, and the last, flying boats it would ever fly. 'I went on two proving flights for the flying boats and was stewardess on the first passenger service. It took four and a half days to fly from Southampton to Johannesburg, but after the Dakotas the flying boats were a revelation. There was simply no comparison. The flying boats had everything.

'My routine was to go to Buckingham Palace Road in central London at 6.30 in the morning. By seven the passengers would have arrived. They would then be put on buses and I'd join them at the front of the bus for the journey to the south coast. We'd stop at the Hog's Back on the way for breakfast' –

OLIVE CARLISLE

Olive Carlisle with the vast array of
equipment and utensils for which she
was held personally responsible.

A Short Solent flying boat circles in before touchdown.

the famous hotel on the Hog's Back road near Farnham in Surrey. 'The total journey time to Southampton was two hours – not bad when you think there were no motorways, though of course there was very little traffic in those days. By the time we arrived the passengers would have all got to know each other. Passengers then were always more ready to get to know each other, partly I think because there were fewer of them, partly because they had more time and partly because they were excited and all together in what was still seen as a great adventure. No one really took flying for granted as they do now. The passengers would really be like children on an outing – all keyed up, almost bubbling with excitement. Some of the military people we flew were regulars but for most – particularly those emigrating – this was likely to be a once in a lifetime experience. In most cases they never expected to return to England.

'When we got to Southampton I would join the steward on the flying boat at Berth 50 while the passengers were taken by the traffic officers through emigration and customs. The flying boats by this time were pulled up to the berth so we didn't need the launches there any more.'

Olive's memory of what it was like to travel on a flying boat is extraordinarily detailed. She admits this has a great deal to do with the fact that she enjoyed the work so much, but it is also because she was a keen record keeper who hung on to leaflets, advertisements and pretty much anything else she could lay her hands on. In those days every passenger, when the aircraft crossed the Equator, received an ornate crossing the line certificate signed by the captain.

This, then, was what it was like to step onto one of those long-vanished Short Solents.

'Passengers boarded from the starboard side and first reached the promenade deck, which had windows either side and a bar. It was here that they could walk up and down any time during the flight, to have a smoke and a drink and stretch their legs. The windows were long rather than wide so you could see down to the scene below. There were no seats on the promenade deck and it was about 12 feet by 8 or thereabouts with a clock and maps on the wall. The Solent's interior was much more like a sumptuous hotel lounge than the cabin of a plane. In addition to the bar on the prom there was a bar upstairs. From the promenade deck a

door led to the Ladies' Room which had two big mirrors, seats and expensive cosmetics. Forward of the promenade deck you reached a staircase which led up to the upstairs seating, and further forward was the library and the Men's Cloakroom. Beyond this there were two cabins each with six seats or, on some flying boats, beds.

'On take-off or landing the stewards fastened bulkheads to doors separating the two downstairs cabins so that if water came on board it could be contained. Right at the front was a room for parcels and mail. Everything I've described – Ladies' Room, promenade, cabins and so on – was underneath the flight deck. We carried thirty-four passengers and later thirty-nine, with about twelve on the bottom deck and seventeen on the top. They sat four to

COMFORT
TO THE CAPE

Comfort has always been the keynote of travel in a flying-boat, and the two spacious decks of the Short Solent flying-boat set new standards for the satisfaction of passengers. Placed on B.O.A.C.'s London—Johannesburg service on May 4, the Solent carries thirty-four passengers, on two decks. The upper deck cabin, illustrated on this page, has twelve seats arranged in groups, and the three lower deck cabins are arranged in a similar fashion. Generous-sized windows give an excellent view from the seats, which are fully adjustable. Appropriately enough in a flying-boat the seats are in blue, with a darker blue for the carpets ; the upper part of the walls and the curtains are in two shades of beige ; cunningly concealed lighting adds to the luxurious styling of the cabins.

DRAWINGS P
HAROLD BU
Copyr
THE AERO

OLIVE CARLISLE

80

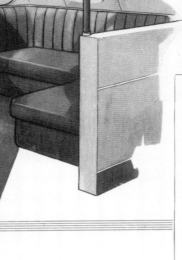

STEWARDESS

81

(Top left). Spaciously designed, the ladies' dressing-room has two dressing-tables and is excellently fitted out, with lighted mirrors and all that might be required.

(Top right). The entry door can be seen at the aft end of the promenade deck. On the right is the foot of the companion-way.

(Below left). Looking aft in the main cabin on the upper deck, which has twelve adjustable seats. The bar is behind the partition at the far end.

(Left). The bar and lounge seat at the top of the companion-way. There is also a fully equipped galley.

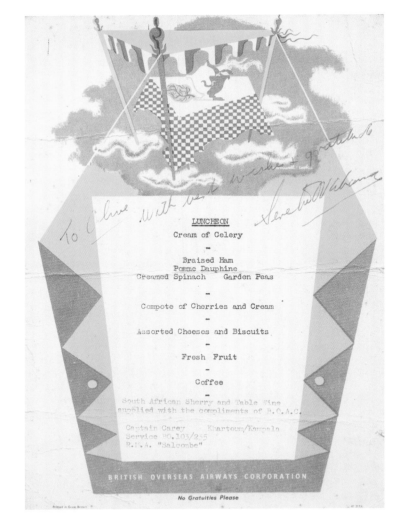

To Olive With best wishes & gratitude
[signature]

LUNCHEON

Cream of Celery

–

Braised Ham
Pomme Dauphine
Creamed Spinach   Garden Peas

–

Compote of Cherries and Cream

–

Assorted Cheeses and Biscuits

–

Fresh Fruit

–

Coffee

–

South African Sherry and Table Wine
supplied with the compliments of B.O.A.C.

Captain Carey   Khartoum/Kampala
Service No.103/245
B.S.A. "Salcombe"

BRITISH OVERSEAS AIRWAYS CORPORATION

No Gratuities Please

'But the flying boats were also worked very hard which meant that the flight engineers sometimes had their work cut out to keep them in the air. Apart from the fact that they might break down in remote parts of the world, repairs had to be carried out on what might be a wave-tossed lake or river estuary.

'We often had engine changes and as this might happen anywhere the engines sometimes had to be flown out to us. I remember we were stuck in Karachi once for three days waiting for an engine. And of course the actual business of working on an engine – or replacing one – was immensely difficult because the poor old engineer officer had to get on the wing or under the engine to work on it from a boat that was constantly going up and down.'

For the journey to Johannesburg the flying boat would reach Augusta in Sicily on the first day, or Marseille if the weather was bad. Olive recalls that as they flew in to Augusta the captain would almost always entertain the passengers by flying around Mount Etna. From Augusta the next leg was to Cairo, flying along the North African coast, past the site of many battlefields from the Desert War.

'This was an extraordinary experience,' explains Olive, 'because for mile after mile you could see the remains of tanks and armoured cars, dugout trenches and other signs of battle. It was dry in the desert so none of the remains disappeared or decayed even into the 1950s. A little further out to sea you could also see with absolute clarity all the ships lying sunk in the shallow Mediterranean.'

At Cairo passengers and crew would lunch together on a boat on the Nile and then fly on to Luxor to stay the night. As the passengers were taken out by launch in the morning they would see the sun rising over the great river.

'That was one of the highlights of the whole trip,' says Olive. 'Unless you've seen it you can't imagine how wonderful and romantic it is.'

Less romantic were the cooking arrangements on the flying boats, but the stewardesses were not expected to slave over a hot stove.

'The flying boats had a clever electrical Crittal Oven but this was strictly the preserve of the steward, who did all the cooking – the menus could be very good indeed, with four courses freshly cooked.'

Of course looking after the passengers was only part of the job and, as Olive explains, there was plenty of time for fun.

'We used to tease the passengers and tell them that when we crossed the Equator they would feel a bump, and when we were roughly there the captain would deliberately make the plane dip or judder a bit. Some passengers even fell for it!

'We once flew Sir Malcolm Sargent to South Africa, in 1948, and he bought a straw hat for himself and one for me. He then dared me to wear it while I was working behind the bar. Most of the passengers took pictures of me – they thought it was very funny, but another member of the crew warned me and said, "If anyone back at HQ finds out you'll be sacked." And he wasn't joking!

'Another time we were staying in the Silver Springs Hotel at Lake Victoria – which was the next night stop after Luxor. One of the crew had his uniform stolen – someone had pushed a wire down through a window and hooked jacket, trousers and shirt out through the window. Everyone had to chip in bits of clothing or he'd have been really stuck!

'From Lake Victoria we went on to Victoria Falls and then Johannesburg where we landed on the Vaal Dam just south of the city. The passengers then went on by bus. At this time there were only two flights a week to South Africa and

THE CRITTALL
"AIRBORNE" OVEN
(SERIES I)

INSTRUCTIONS TO STEWARDS

BRITISH OVERSEAS AIRWAYS CORPORATION

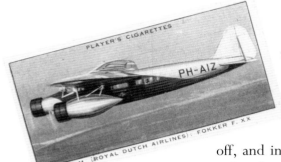

take-offs and arrivals were something of an event — crowds of people gathered and cheered as we landed and took off.

'For a while the flying boat service was interrupted because the floats on the wings kept breaking off, and in the meantime I flew to Australia on Constellations. That was another first for me — I was the first stewardess to fly on them. Then I flew on Argonauts for a while. Both the Constellations and Argonauts flew from Heathrow to Nairobi and South Africa.

'I'd married a flight engineer by now, and a woman was supposed to resign when she got married, but they told me they'd turn a blind eye, so I kept working till 1954 when we decided to start a family.

'While we both still worked we used to communicate across whole continents — I would leave a message at a station in Africa for Andy saying, "I've ordered the milk for Tuesday!"

'One of the funniest incidents I remember was in Karachi where my husband and I used occasionally to cross paths. My husband got to the hotel first and said to someone we called Mr Contractor, a Pakistani gentleman who more or less ran the hotel, "Don't worry about a room for me. I'll share with the incoming stewardess." Mr Contractor immediately replied, "Oh, I don't think BOAC would like that." "But we're married," said my husband. "Oh, I still don't think BOAC would like it!" came the reply. When a similar incident occurred in Rome, the receptionist said, "Bravo!"

'I enjoyed my flying days enormously but after seven years I thought it was time for a change. One of my saddest memories is of young Prince Faisal from the Middle East who flew with us regularly as a child. I liked him very much and got to know him well, but six months after I last said goodbye to him I heard he'd been assassinated along with the rest of his family.'

OLIVE CARLISLE

86

SEASONLESS AND INDETERMINATE AIR

On May 10 at noon precisely our plane took off from Heath Row aerodrome. It is a measure of the newness which still infects air travel that, although once in the air it completes a journey between two points with the utmost dispatch, at the same time it condemns travellers to dreary hours of waiting and preparation on the ground; to tiresome formalities with Customs, Exchange and Immigration controls at all kinds of places, and finally to cumbersome and ponderous journeys by road to and from aerodromes. It took us two hours, after leaving Victoria, to get into the air. But once in the air, no one could have had any complaints over the speed at which we travelled.

I do not know what my twenty companions were thinking as we took off, but once again I was struck by the brutal, impersonal quality of this form of departure. I have never ceased to be touched in some indefinable way by a ship casting off and moving out to sea. There is something symbolic about it to which the hungry, starved rationalism of our twentieth-century

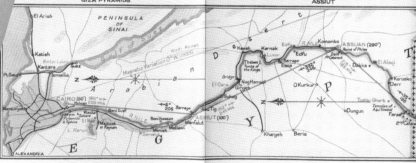

GIZA PYRAMIDS

ASSIUT

CAIRO AND THE PYRAMIDS

From Cairo you fly due south and follow closely the Valley of the Nile. You may see beneath you to the west the Giza Pyramids, the largest of which (Cheops) is nearly 500 feet in height : then further south the ancient step pyramid of Sakara, built some 5,000 years ago by King Zoser. Further on again, to the west, lies Lake Karun, and next to it the fertile oases of Fayum

ASSIUT AND ITS BARRAGE

Your next stop, Assiut, is famous for its Barrage across the Nile, which here turns away from our course in a vast loop.

Far to the left you pass Luxor, and almost beneath you lies Thebes, with its Tombs of the Kings (the site of the Tutankhamen excavations) and the twin Memnon Colossi of Amenhotep III and his Consort

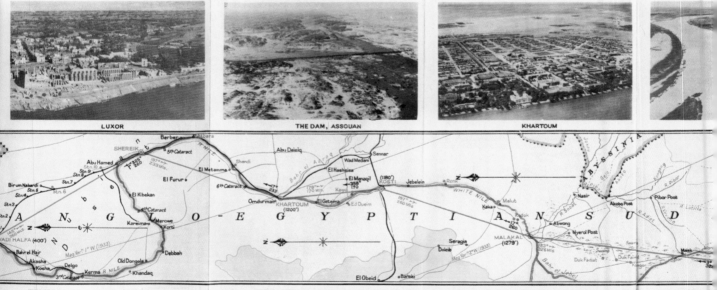

DEUTSCHE LUFT HANSA: DORNIER DO. 18 FLYING-BOAT

mind instantly and inevitably responds. The ship is of the authentic, antique material of the imagination. Even at a railway station, the flutter of a handkerchief, the wave of a hand or a face looking back at one from a window, to some extent redeems the train's impersonal yet hysterical departure. The aeroplane makes none of these concessions. There is no interval between the 'being here' and the 'going there' — the two conditions are created, as it were, with one stroke of the knife, and one is left with a vague, uncomprehended sense of shock. One feels as if one had been subjected to a lightning amputation.

At one moment we were in England in the spring, and at the next we were above it in seasonless and indeterminate air. We climbed quickly. One familiar landmark after another slid into view with a certain irrevocable ease and then floated out of sight behind us. We had not been up many minutes when I noticed with dismay that we were already coming over the South Downs. It was not until that moment that I realized fully the enormity of the accomplished break.

Some children began to play in the plane. There was a little girl with the old-young face of the European child in Africa. Over her shoulder was slung a

LUXOR

THE DAM, ASSOUAN

KHARTOUM

TEMPLES OF LUXOR AND KARNAK

These famous remains, as well as the Temples of Luxor and Karnak and Sethos, are actually best approached from your next stop (Assouan). Before reaching Assouan, however, you will fly across a rugged gorge, faced by black basalt hills, and a little later you will see the Nile again and the Railway which follows it along its Eastern side from Luxor

THE GREAT ASSOUAN DAM

Assouan, with its celebrated dam of 2,000 yards in length which links up a knot of Islets (the 1st Cataract) is, from the point of view of scenery, most interesting, and is also notable for the Ruins of Philæ, whose temples during the winter are submerged. From here you follow the Nile past the great Rock Temple of Abu Simnel as far as Wadi Halfa

KHARTOUM, KITCHENER AND OMDURMAN

Here you enter the Sudan, leaving the Nile to the West until you reach Abu Hamed

You will land first at Shereik and again at Khartoum. This is the capital of the Sudan—a city rebuilt by Kitchener, after his victory at Omdurman, in the form of the Union Flag, as a perpetual reminder of the British Empire

THE BE

It is in this area begins. You will as Kosti

Your approach by the appearan elephants may so over them

leopard-skin bag, and I could tell almost for sure at which shop in Nairobi she had bought it. There was a little boy wearing the colours of a well-known preparatory school in Southern Rhodesia, already a little white master of everything except himself. And there were the parents with the strained, set official faces that one knows from experience will only become warm and smiling, in Africa, with sunset and the sun downer.

The man in front of me was a plumber from Birmingham. He had heard that the mines in Johannesburg were short of plumbers so he had taken a few weeks off, at his own expense, to look at conditions. If he liked it, he would settle in South Africa for good. Despite all the money he made, he did not like post-war Britain; 'too cramped', he said, 'too many restrictions'. I thought to myself: 'There he is, the Pilgrim Father, 1949 model, complete with motive.'

There was a young surveyor still wearing Varsity flannels and a brown tweed coat, pleased and thrilled to be on his way to work for the Colonial Survey Department in the neighbourhood of Tabora. There was a businessman from Tanganyika; strangely he looked more like a certain general, under whom I had served, than the general did himself.

THE CRATER, KILIMANJARO

MALAKAL

JUBA

KISUMU
↓
NAIROBI
↓
SALISBURY
↓
1607 MILES

AeroShell is refined by a scientific process which gives it all the advantages of Castor Oil (an extra reserve of lubrication) with none of its disadvantages, such as messy engines, greasy valves and hard carbon deposit.

...NING OF THE BUSH
: the desert ends and tropical growth
er long stretches of bush as far south

he air port of Malakal is indicated
f vast swamps in which herds of
nes be seen stampeding as you fly

NEW CAPITAL OF MONGALLA PROVINCE
The swamp ends at Juba. This is the new Capital of Mongalla Province, and the terminus of the traffic on the White Nile. Here are good motor car routes in all directions. The ground begins to rise, and a great variety of game may be seen. You next come to Entebbe the Capital of Uganda, and then to Kisumu on the beautiful Lake Victoria.

KENYA COLONY, AND BIG GAME
Your next stop, Nairobi, is the Capital of Kenya Colony and here game of every kind abounds. From Nairobi the next stop is Moshi which lies in the middle of the great Tanganyika coffee belt on the southern slopes of Kilimanjaro, the highest mountain in Africa (19,710 feet) whose summit capped with snow may under favourable conditions be seen from the air.

MOUNTAIN SCENERY
Moshi and its great mountain are soon le... Dodoma is reached. Mbeya, the next stop is... that it is one of the highest stations on the... far from here are situated the new Lupa G... the South bound service Mbeya is the la... Tanganyika Territory.

There was a Director of Agriculture, a nice man with a record of devoted service, but already assuming, with a certain relief one suspected, some of the importance that would descend on him at his destination. There were some other officials returning from leave; an army sister on her way to Eritrea; a missionary and his wife on the way back to Uganda; and two commercial travellers, in the grand manner, dressed just a little too well for the occasion. The plane itself was being flown by a South African crew. It was a well-known, popular, much-advertised American model, which I personally rather dislike. It is fast and reliable, and technically, I am sure, a very good machine. But it is designed, like so many American aircraft, with only one aim: to hurl through the air, as fast as possible, the maximum number of people. I longed for the slower, more comfortable British flying boats with their obstinate, old-fashioned respect for privacy and individual needs.

By the time lunch was served we were high over Paris. The lunch dealt another blow to the memory of Europe. Everything – the meat, the fruit, the salads – was South African, with the sharp, almost metallic tang of the typical Southern African product. The people who served it had an equivalent tang in

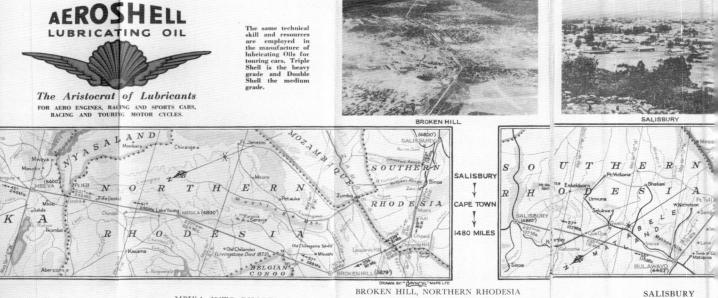

BROKEN HILL

SALISBURY

SALISBURY
↑
CAPE TOWN
↑
1480 MILES

BROKEN HILL, NORTHERN RHODESIA

DRAWN BY "DAYNOIL" MAPS LTD

...AIN SCENERY

...ountain are soon left behind and ...ya, the next stop is of interest in ...est stations on the route. Not ...d the new Lupa Goldfields. On ...e Mbeya is the last station in

MPIKA INTO RHODESIA

You next land at Mpika, the centre of a celebrated big-game area. Your flight from here is over dense bush and occasional clearings in which you may see herds of game. You now cross Rhodesia to the centre of Luanga —a district extremely rich in minerals.

BROKEN HILL, NORTHERN RHODESIA

Broken Hill, where you will land next, was named after the well-known Australian mining town

Broken Hill is famous not only for its mine, whose workings are visible from the air, but also as being the site of one of the oldest human skulls in the world (homorhodesiensis) now in the British Museum

SALISBURY

Salisbury is the Capital of Southern R... here you will pass over the cattle plains ... and so to Bulawayo from where, if you ... fly to the Victoria Falls in a matter ... Leaving Bulawayo you will get a view ... Matopo Hills where Cecil Rhodes lies bu... cross the Limpopo and enter the Union o...

their voices; as I looked at them I suddenly realized that the world of modern travel is very small. Living in London or Paris, unless one plans carefully, it is difficult to see enough of one's friends. But on the highways and skyways of the world one meets and re-meets the same faces. Even I recognized several of the crew with whom I had travelled before.

I was not surprised, therefore, when the captain of the aircraft, as he came down the plane towards me, looked like someone I had seen before. But I was startled a minute later when he stopped by me and said laughingly, 'You don't still think I am a German?'

I recognized him instantly. His name was Jakobus Gerhardus van Waveren. He had been to school with me, was three years my junior and came of an old Free State family. As a pilot he had come to my rescue once during the war in Abyssinia.

'I hardly thought it could be you,' Jakobus Gerhardus now said, 'when I saw your name on the passenger list. I thought the Japanese did for you. I read your obituary notices in the papers years ago. Are you going home? What do you think of my new kite?'

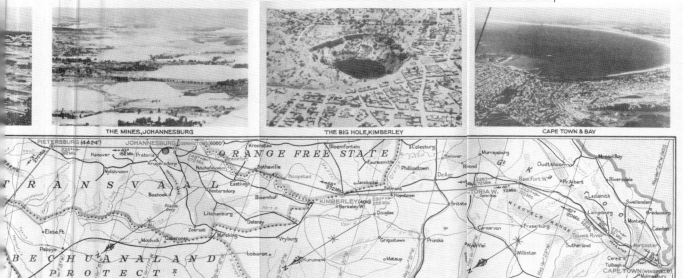

THE MINES, JOHANNESBURG

THE BIG HOLE, KIMBERLEY

CAPE TOWN & BAY

PRETORIA AND JOHANNESBURG

Not long after leaving Pietersburg you will be approaching the great Premier Mine—which you will see from the air—where the famous Cullinan diamond was discovered, and Pretoria, the Administrative Capital of the Union. Your next stop is Johannesburg the highest aerodrome on the route—5,700 feet above sea level. The city is the largest in Africa, south of Cairo.

KIMBERLEY-DIAMONDS.

Leaving Johannesburg the high grounds fall gradually until you reach the plains of the Orange Free State. Here you will land at Kimberley, the home of the South African Diamond, and famous for its " Big Hole." The city itself is irregular in layout, owing to its gradual development out of the old mining camp. Ostriches may often be seen on the plains between here and the next stop (Victoria West) whence you traverse the bleached and parched plains of the Karroo

THE END OF THE JOURNEY, AND CAPE TOWN

From the plains of the Karroo you climb over the picturesque Hex River mountains which at close range are seen to be trellised on their southern slopes with vines, stretching south as far as the Great Table Mountain of your last stop, Cape Town. This is the legislative Capital of the Union of South Africa, and from here there are traffic connections in every direction, by sea, land or air

91

I was tremendously pleased to see him, and I enjoyed to the full this moment of being with someone whom I had known when I was young. He had a rich fund of information, about persons whom I had not seen for years.

He then jumped up suddenly and said, 'Come and look at my kite.' I followed him silently into the cockpit.

We were well over France. Grenoble was just coming up under the starboard wing. The air was blue, cool and clear. Suddenly the peak of Mont Blanc, not white but a deep, golden colour, came out of the haze of the horizon. It lifted its head like the muzzle of a great polar bear sniffing the air for news of ice.

'Seldom see it like that!' the pilot shouted in my ear. 'It's obviously your lucky day.'

'Look, the Alps,' he called again. And there they were far to the east, a remote vision of snow, ice and celestial blue, their sharp white peaks gently brushed every now and then by the tip of a long, aluminium wing. A kind of hush, an involuntary silence seemed to spread from them into the plane. At the back, people became quiet, observing an unofficial minute's silence, as it were, for that dead world, that other kingdom of snow. Hard by on a ledge, I could distinctly see a small military cemetery with a large tricolour flying over it. I thought I recognized one of the many sad cemeteries of Resistance dead that there are everywhere in those hills.

And now the golden, the rich, the fertile valleys of France fell away from us, that fruitful sun-drenched earth responding so warmly to the spring and to thousands of years of love, care and civilized attention. A long series of peaks, broken and jagged, too low for snow and too high for human cultivation, tossed us about like a lifeboat on a stormy sea. We came out into the still air over Cagnes. A speedboat was laying across the bay a curve of foam that looked on that sea so blue and still, more like a smoke-screen across a noonday sky. A long way behind us a plume of snow sank gently into the afternoon haze.

A steward called us for tea. I had forgotten how well and how much my countrymen eat. The plumber, leaning back over his chair, asked me if everybody ate like that in South Africa.

I said, 'Yes, most white people do.' And he said, 'Crikey!'

Over Corsica, afternoon was turning into evening. The ravines, which were deep, narrow clefts in the flanks of steep mountains, began to fill with purple shadow. The shadows of the peaks themselves lengthened and sped forward eagerly towards the distant sea; one sharp, volcanic cone threw its bar of darkness right across a wide plain which was still gold and gold-green with sunlight. The first golden line of Africa appeared in front of us just as the sun began to sink rapidly towards the horizon. Were it not for that hour and for that light, such a vast quantity of sand would have looked desolate and dull.

The plumber was obviously dismayed and disappointed.

'Is that the actual coast of Africa?' he asked.

'Yes, technically,' I said, trying to comfort him. 'But you will hardly think so when you come back.'

Were it not for the difficulties of speech in these planes, I would have tried to explain that what we were looking at was in the first place Mediterranean; secondly Levantine; thirdly Oriental; and only then, by the blind grace of geography, African. The more one knows of Africa, the less one feels this northern end to be part of it and the more one knows the Mediterranean the more one sees its continuity even on these bleached and sandy shores of Northern Africa.

We landed at Castel Benito in time for dinner. But that same morning, only eight hours before, we had been in Britain and in the spring.

Venture to the Interior, Laurens van der Post, 1954

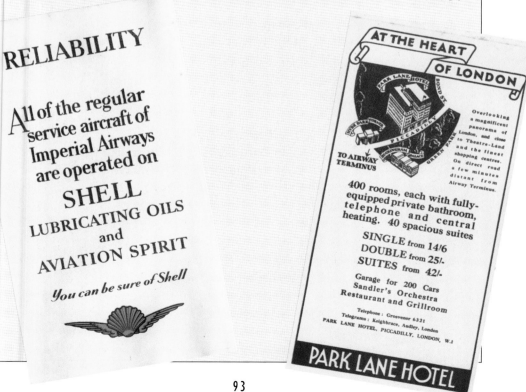

Edward Hulton's preserved Short Sunderland taking off from Windermere in the Lake District in 1979.

KEN EMMOTT
PILOT

Ken Emmott knew he wanted to fly from the day his father took him from the family home in Burnley, Lancashire to Blackpool. Among the myriad entertainments one caught his eye: the chance for a five-minute flight in a Sopwith Camel, the World War I biplane fighter that had pioneered aerial warfare above the Western Front. It was irresistible, as he explains.

'They were giving rides in the plane from Blackpool Sands and I'd have been about seven. I loved it. I remember the pilot was a veteran of the Great War and he took me up with my two cousins. It was crowded in that little plane and there were no seat belts, but it was a wonderful sensation. From that moment I wanted to be an airman. Mind you, at that time you were very lucky if you could get into flying – it was for the privileged few.'

Ken was just eighteen in 1939 when war broke out and he knew that his best chance of becoming a pilot was to join up now. He'd won a place at Nottingham University, but knew he would be called up before he had any chance of completing the college course so he volunteered. 'If you wanted to go in the Air Force at that time you needed to be good at maths, and I was really good at maths so I walked the exam. I think I probably got 100 per cent – the questions just seemed really easy to me. The medical was tough, too, but I had no problems. Once accepted you were sent to what was called a grading school to test your abilities. The test basically involved flying a Tiger Moth for eight or nine hours – an instructor kept an eye on you throughout this period and as a result it was decided that I should be a pilot. I was then sent to Lord's Cricket Ground in London, of all places. To this day I still don't really know precisely why I was selected to be a pilot rather than, say, a navigator or radio operator, but I was very happy with the decision.'

Together with hundreds of other young recruits Ken stayed at Lord's just long enough to be kitted out with his uniform and inoculated against a range of tropical diseases. He was then sent to the Initial Training Wing at Newquay in Cornwall.

'This was what we called ground school – here you learned navigation and a great deal of theory. From Ground School we were sent to a place near Leicester for more practical flying experience on Tiger Moths. After this whirlwind series of training moves I was sent to America. The reason was that the weather was better in America – all those clear blue skies – and it was well out of the conflict that raged over Europe. Of course, being America, they also had the most tremendous facilities.'

When trainee pilots were sent out from England they were assigned either to the US Army Air Corps or to the US Navy Air Corps. Ken went with the Navy and was sent to Pensacola in Florida, where he was to spend the next nine months.

'They had three airfields on the base as well as a flying boat base with a number of Catalina flying boats. Money was definitely no object. I flew a plane called a Spartan before going on to the Stearman, a fast biplane, and then on to what was called a Vultee monoplane. Everyone in those days started on biplanes and from there we graduated to flying boats. We did a total of 200 hours' flying at Pensacola. But at each stage it was possible to fail the whole thing. After eight hours on a biplane the instructor would tell you if he felt you could now fly solo – he'd then get out of the plane and let you do a circuit, and woe betide you if you made a mess of it. We also had to learn to fly in formation. There isn't much difference between a mono- and a biplane other than that, generally speaking, the biplane can fly more slowly. But RAF training on all these planes was the perfect grounding for later civilian flying.'

From Pensacola Ken was sent to Prince Edward Island in Canada. The course here was a general RAF reconnaissance course designed to teach navigation, bomb aiming, the ins and outs of machine guns and how to use them, and ship identification.

'We used Ansons for this,' explains Ken. 'They were ancient planes even at this time but it's worth remembering that when the first 1000-bomber raid was sent out over Berlin, some of the planes were Ansons. Which is amazing when you consider that the Anson was basically an old cloth-covered plane. I was at Prince Edward Island for two months before returning to the UK. From there I was immediately sent to India as a copilot.

'I spent the next six months doing anti-submarine work – flying around

KEN EMMOTT

98

Qantas Catalina flying boat *Vega* being towed to her moorings at Kogalla, Ceylon.

IWM CH 14949

watching convoys of ships and with three depth charges ready under each wing if we sighted any German submarines. We never sighted a target but if we had, the technique was to drop the depth charges in a sort of diagonal line across the presumed path of the sub. You didn't have to hit the sub to disable it — if the depth charge exploded close enough to the relatively thin metal plates of the subs' body it would damage it. German subs operated all round India, South Africa and Gibraltar.

'As copilot I found myself mostly flying the plane once we'd taken off — the captain usually did the take-off and landing and then left it to me. Other than that we did one hour off and one on, each relieving the other. On those Catalinas a patrol would be twenty-four hours. We had nine crew — a pilot, copilot, two flight engineers, one navigator and a team of air gunners.'

The Catalina was a high-winged aircraft — the idea being that the high wings kept the engines clear of the spray. One engineer sat in what was called the tower, above the main fuselage but below the wing.

By 1943 Ken was at Lough Erne in Ireland, where he was put through a captain's course that lasted three months. After that the RAF gave him his own flying boat.

'I was just twenty. And that speed of promotion could never have hap-

PLAYER'S CIGARETTES

EASTERN AIRLINES: LOCKHEED "ELECTRA"

KEN EMMOTT

pened in peacetime. I was given a new crew and we were based at Oban in Scotland. We then had to get ourselves and our Catalina ready to join a squadron. All that really happened was that we checked the plane over and practised flying it. As soon as we felt comfortable with the whole thing we flew the plane out to India. The Mediterranean had opened up by now, but our first leg took us out into the Atlantic at night and then swinging in towards Gibraltar.

'At Gibraltar the aircraft was serviced before we continued on through the Mediterranean to Bitter Lakes on the Suez Canal, then on to Al Habbaniyah in Iraq. My crew all fell sick there so we stayed for eight days. Curiously, whatever it was that knocked them flat had no effect at all on me. From there we flew to Bahrain and then Karachi. We joined a squadron there that was operating on convoy escorts – following ships round from Bombay, Ceylon and Madras. That lasted two years. Then I got fed up with it so I volunteered for a special duty squadron on Liberators, a land-plane. We were trained on the new plane at Bangalore and then started operational flying from China Bay in Ceylon. I stayed there flying long-range missions until the end of the war. We were mostly dropping guerrillas, guns, radios and special troops in the Malayan peninsula to fight the Japanese. It was ironic, too, because after the Americans dropped their bombs on Hiroshima and Nagasaki, the authorities decided that the troops we'd been supplying were actually nasty Communists so we started dropping Gurkhas in to fight the special troops we'd supplied earlier.

'We also started dropping medical supplies and doctors into former prison camps. We often hear about the refusal of the Japanese to surrender but they did give in here and there – or most of them did – once the Emperor told them to. I can remember dropping medical supplies into a prison camp at Medan in Northern Sumatra. Here the local Japanese leader had been told to take the propellers off his aircraft and there they all were: 140 aeroplanes lined up at the edge of the runway and every one with its propeller removed. My last trip was to pick up British prisoners of war from Singapore and return them to Ceylon – all I can remember is what a terrible state they were in.

'The Liberator I flew at that time was unusual in that it hadn't been painted with camouflage paint like all the other planes in the squadron – that was a bit scary because it was bright silver and could be seen from outer space! But the lack of paint actually meant it could travel 5 knots faster than all the other planes!

'After my last mission I flew that plane to Cawnpore and I remember the marshaller – the man who signalled to us where to go once we were on the

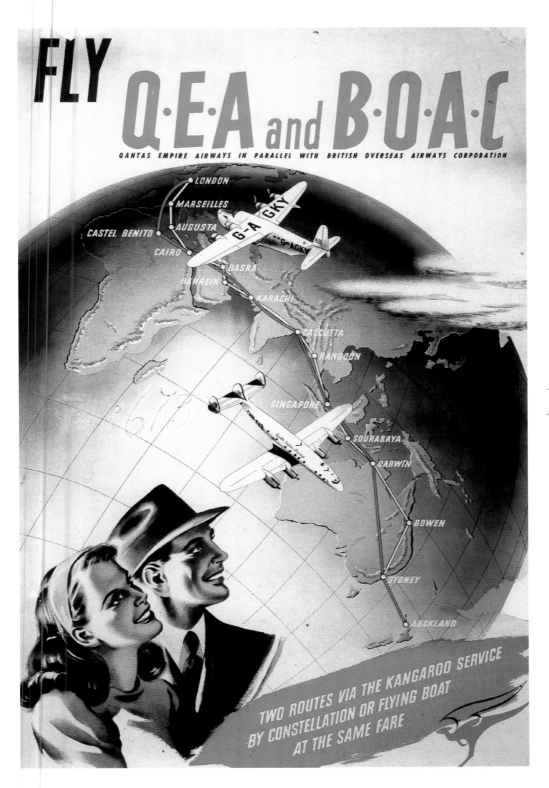

PILOT

101

ground – directed me into thick bush. Once the plane was well hidden I just left it there, and like thousands of other planes all over India it was just abandoned. Many flying boats were just sunk and of course hundreds of pilots suddenly found they had nothing to do. I went back to the UK and heard that BOAC were looking for pilots.'

Ken was lucky. He was immediately taken on by BOAC and by the end of 1946 he was piloting a Hythe flying boat for the company's new passenger service. The Hythe was a civilian version of the Sunderland flying boat. It had seats for passengers although by comparison with a modern passenger plane it was all pretty spartan.

'There were tables and a bar and plenty of room,' explains Ken – 'I seem to remember people wandering about as if they were at a party! The Hythe carried a maximum of thirty-five passengers and we were based at Poole.'

After his time flying all over the world Ken was enormously confident about his new role, and his confidence was matched by a general feeling in BOAC and other civilian airlines that they were at the beginning of a huge revolution in travel. But on a more mundane level pilots and other crew simply got on with the job.

'A typical day for a pilot would start with a weather check – you needed to know what to expect right along whichever route you were to take. Having sorted that out you'd study the route and work out how much fuel you would need. You'd then make a flight plan as well as checking on your passengers. You and your crew would then be taken out to the flying boat by launch. The crew would get the plane ready for flight by running through checks on all the equipment – this series of checks was very simple on the Sunderland compared to, say, the last plane I flew before I retired, which was a 747 Jumbo jet.

'The passengers were brought out after the crew and then we'd get the engines started. As soon as two of the four engines were going and had been checked the radio officer would cast off – he'd operate the lever that released the wire that held us to the buoy. We'd then start the other two engines while taxiing into the take-off position. We always used full power for take-off and a Sunderland would need to reach about 90 knots to take off. Compare that with a Boeing 747 which would need to reach 170 knots!'

Early flights from Poole were to Singapore, Australia, Hong Kong, Japan or Johannesburg, via various intermediate stops. Poole to Singapore would take you via Bordeaux, Marseille, Bahrain, Karachi, Calcutta and Rangoon. Sunderlands could fly several hours at a stretch and in that time they might cover 1200 miles.

KEN EMMOTT

'They used to say that the pilot of a flying boat was like a one-armed wallpaper hanger,' says Ken with a grin. 'The wheels on a land plane made it easy to go straight, but on a flying boat the torque of the engines going round one way pushes the plane the other way. The effect is to make the flying boat swing sideways, and that tendency could be made a lot worse by crosswinds which were a frequent problem. To avoid the tendency to swing sideways the pilot had to use rudder and differential engines – it was a skilful business involving the rudders, ailerons, and elevators, but usually did the trick.

One of many young women who volunteered to do wartime work with BOAC being trained as a coxswain for flying boat launches.   IWM CH 14051

'Porpoising was another problem unique to flying boats: as you can imagine, when you're taking off across water there are forces under the flying boat that you wouldn't get with a land plane. These forces tend to shift from the back of the aeroplane to the front. Our manual explained that if the flying boat starts to porpoise but you still manage to get into the air the plane may well leave the water for just a few seconds and then hit it again – and it may do it with such a bang that you could lose an engine. So at the first hint of porpoising you were supposed to hold a backward force on the control column – that usually did the trick.

'A Sunderland had a draught of 5 feet 6 inches, which meant that the plane had to rise up out of the water until it was "planing" – only the bottom of the fuselage touching the water, until it gained flying speed.

'Over the years I had lots of engine failures on Sunderlands, but we were trained to fly on three

An Indian guard at the marine airport at Karachi stands beneath a long distance signpost.   IWM CH 14021

The New Comet Airliner
ROLLS - ROYCE AVON JET ENGINES

will surpass every other aircraft for world travel

Cruising at 500 miles an hour in an atmosphere of incomparable comfort with a smoothness and quietude hitherto unexampled the Comet passenger will fly the great intercontinental stages of the world in a few hours. Jet speed shortens the journey and jet smoothness makes it seem shorter still—one arrives without the feeling of having travelled.

DE HAVILLAND OF GREAT BRITAIN

engines and it wasn't actually that difficult to do. Luckily I never lost more than one engine. Engine loss is serious but not catastrophic so long as you know how to handle it. With one engine gone the plane will try to swerve, so you counteract that tendency with lots of rudder and rudder trim. The biggest problem flying on three engines is that the plane just isn't as efficient as it should be.

'The only other problem that I had to cope with now and then was really bad weather, by which I mean weather so bad that you couldn't land where you were scheduled to land and so had to hunt around for an alternative. If that was impossible you just circled above the place you were supposed to land for an hour or so hoping that conditions would improve – that's why it was a rule that you had to have at least an hour's fuel on top of what was needed to get you where you were going, as well as fuel to an alternative destination.

'The Sunderlands eventually packed up in 1950. I'd flown them from 1946 until the end as a copilot. I was then sent to fly with the Comet jet development unit. The Comet really was a huge change from everything that had gone before. There had been military jets up to then but the Comet was the first jet developed for passenger flying. Its powered controls were basically the same as the controls on the Sunderlands, but the technique for flying was totally different because a jet engine is totally different from a propeller engine. With a propeller the air is driven backwards over the wings, the aircraft moves forward and gets lift from the wings. With the jet engine air isn't pushed over the wings in the same way so there's no direct lift as there is with the propeller. So you get a more rapid response from a propeller engine.

'There was no problem with the Comet's engines, but there were serious problems early on with its fuselage. Three Comets crashed and after a lot of research they discovered that what was happening was that the ADF window – actually a metal plate – was coming off, which meant the cabin lost all pressure and the whole of the top of the cabin was torn off.

'In 1954 I started to fly Constellations – these were four-engined aircraft and absolutely lovely to handle. The main vice of an aircraft is what we call high wing loading. If the wing loading is high the aircraft will always need careful handling – by careful handling I mean you can't afford to lose speed at all. The Constellation was far more tolerant and a real pleasure to fly. During my Constellation days I was still flying diplomats and military people around but there were more businessmen now and celebrities, even royalty. I flew Princess Margaret, for example, as well as Frank Sinatra and Clement Atlee. By now the interior of passenger planes, but particularly the Constellations, was far more comfortable – even, I suppose you could say, luxurious.'

Ken Emmott flying Edward Hulton's Sunderland: this page after landing at Chatham on the Medway 1984; opposite top, the Sunderland touches down at Chatham with Ken at the controls (bottom).

KEN EMMOTT

106

But already Ken could see that jets were the future. In 1958 the Comet, having been modified after its early failures, came back as the Comet Mk 4, which he flew from 1961 until 1965. Jets did, however, have some things in common with earlier aircraft. 'All planes, whether the old flying boats, biplanes or modern jets today, require the attention of both pilot and copilot when they are taking off and landing, but these days once you are airborne you go onto autopilot. Even the earlier planes had a limited autopilot. On the Catalinas and Constellations they just kept the plane level. Now they can do almost anything.

'In 1965 the Comets were phased out and I started flying 707s – now that was an unforgiving beast! If you did something wrong it really let you know about it. And your landing technique had to be spot on. From 1965 until 1971 I flew 707s all over the world; then 747s. In 1976 I had to retire from British Airways, as the old BOAC had by then become, but I went and flew for Dan Air and then Zambia Airways – the thing about flying is it gets in your blood and you just hate to give it up!

'In the end I was forced to retire for good – or at least I thought it would be for good. I was sixty. It was 1981 and out of the blue I got a phone call from a chap called Edward Hulton, son of the Hulton of *Picture Post* fame. He owned a Sunderland flying boat – probably one of the last still in working order – and wanted someone to fly it. Well, I applied and got the job – largely I suppose because there weren't that many pilots left in the world who knew

how to pilot a flying boat. And I flew that flying boat for ten years — which is strange when you think that my career had as it were come full circle. I started on flying boats and was on a flying boat forty and more years later. It was a bit of a shock going back.

'In the end Edward Hulton sold it to a chap called Kermit Weeks, an American who wanted to learn how to fly a flying boat, so I taught him. With him as my copilot we then flew from Southampton to the USA, via Ireland, Iceland, Labrador, Toronto and then a place called Oshkosh in Wisconsin where the biggest air show in the world is held each year.

'I loved flying that old boat again, but if you pushed me I'd have to say that the plane I loved flying the most was the Boeing 747 — it had power controls and every possible facility a pilot could want, and not a single vice.'

TIMETABLES.

RAL AFRICAN SERVICE

SOUTHBOUND.

...isumu — Nairobi — Lusaka.

	Local Standard Time.	Days of Services.	
		Every	Every
dep.	0800	Tuesday	
arr.	morn.		
dep.	1030	Tuesday	Monday
dep.	1200	"	"
dep.	1415	"	"
arr.	aftn.		
dep.	0630	Wednesday	Tuesday
dep.	0800	"	"
dep.	1025	"	"
arr.	morn.		

NORTHBOUND.

...saka — Nairobi — Kisumu.

	Local Standard Time.	Days of Services.	
		Every	Every
dep.	1000	Wednesday	Thursday
dep.	1050	"	"
dep.	1330	"	"
arr.	aftn.		
dep.	0700	Thursday	Friday
dep.	0950	"	"
dep.	1150	"	"
arr.	aftn.		
dep.	1615	"	"
arr.	even.		

KISUMU—NAIROBI FEEDER SERVICE.

NORTHBOUND.

		Local Standard Time.	Days of Services.	
			Every	Every
Nairobi	dep.	1615	Monday	Friday
Kisumu	arr.	aftn.		

SOUTHBOUND.

		Local Standard Time.	Days of Services.	
			Every	Every
Kisumu	dep.	0800	Wednesday	Sunday
Nairobi	arr.	morn.		

COAST SERVICE

SOUTHBOUND.

		Local Standard Time.	Days of Services.	
			Every	Every
Nairobi	dep.	0740	Sunday	Wednesday
Mombasa	dep.	1100	"	"
Tanga	dep.	1155	"	"
Zanzibar	dep.	1250	"	"
Dar es Salaam	arr.	aftn.		

NORTHBOUND.

		Local Standard Time.	Days of Services.	
			Every	Every
Dar es Salaam	dep.	1115	Monday	Friday
Z...	dep.	1155	"	"
	dep.	1250	"	"
	dep.	1430	"	"
	arr.	aftn.		

HIGHLANDS SERVICE.

NORTHBOUND.

		Local Standard Time.	Days of Services.	
			Every	Every
Nairobi	dep.	1210	Monday	Friday
Nyeri	dep.	1300	"	"
Nanyuki	dep.	1335	"	"
Nakuru	dep.	1435	"	"
Eldoret	dep.	1535	"	"
Kitale	dep.	1615	"	"
Kakamega	dep.	1705	"	"
Kisumu	arr.	aftn.		

SOUTHBOUND.

		Local Standard Time.	Days of Services.	
			Every	Every
Kisumu	dep.	0845	Wednesday	Sunday
Kakamega	dep.	0920	"	"
Kitale	dep.	1010	"	"
Eldoret	dep.	1050	"	"
Nakuru	dep.	1150	"	"
Nanyuki	dep.	1250	"	"
Nyeri	dep.	1325	"	"
Nairobi	arr.	aftn.		

GOLDFIELDS SERVICE

WESTBOUND

Nairobi — Kisumu — Geita.

		Local Standard Time.	Days of Services. Every
Nairobi	... ... dep.	0830	Wednesday
Kisumu	... ... dep.	1040	"
Mara	... ... dep.	1155	"
Musoma	... ... dep.	1240	"
Mwanza	... ... dep.	1400	"
Geita	... ... arr.	aftn.	"

EASTBOUND

Geita — Kisumu — Nairobi.

		Local Standard Time.	Days of Services. Every
Geita	... ... dep.	1100	Thursday
Mwanza	... ... dep.	1155	"
Musoma	... ... dep.	1325	"
Mara	... ... dep.	1410	"
Kisumu	... ... dep.	1530	"
Nairobi	... ... arr.	aftn.	"

CENTRAL TANGANYIKA SERVICE

WESTBOUND.

Dar es Salaam — Morogoro — Dodoma

		Local Standard Time.	Days of Services. Every
Dar es Salaam	... dep.	0830	Monday
Morogoro	... ... dep.	0945	"
Dodoma	... ... arr.	morn.	"

EASTBOUND.

Dodoma — Morogoro — Dar es Salaam

	Local Standard Time.	Days of Services. Every
dep.	1430	Monday
dep.	1615	"
	even.	"

...t Kilosa and
...circum-

WILSON AIRWAYS

TIME-TABLE
IN FORCE FROM JANUA...
1939 UNTIL FURTHER NOT...
This Time-table cancels previous e...
and is subject to alteration without...

WILSON AIRWAYS

TIME-TABLE
...FORCE FROM APRIL 22nd
...UNTIL FURTHER NOTICE
...-table cancels previous editions
...ct to alteration without notice.

FLYING TO BURMA

I flew to Burma in a boat — A boat? Yes, a real boat with mahogany rails and brass fittings and a splendid great bow-wave. And it flew. It was a flying boat.

The beauty of a flying boat is that you land on water. There seems to be a lot of it, and you don't have to cover it with thousands of acres of concrete as you do with good farmland; nor do you need vast administrative offices and hangars. All you need is a lake, or a river, or a sea, or even a reservoir at a pinch, some caravans, a punkah wallah or two, a dog, and of course a cat to arch its back at new arrivals. Then, of course, you have the enthusiastic local populace, black, brown or yellow (and in 1938, respectful), some fast launches to run races with, rafts and buoys and coloured floats, rockets, ropes, cables and other toys — and you are ready to go!

My journey out by flying boat remains one of my happiest memories of travel. We averaged about 2000 miles a day and saw sights enough to fill my head with dreams for the rest of my life. What does the modern traveller see? Nothing but concrete — acres, miles of concrete. Istanbul? Concrete! Samarkand? Concrete. Mandalay? Add corrugated iron. In a modern jet we fly at 35,000 feet, at which height the world of men, with all its beauties and horrors, its triumphs and failures, is only 'an objective'. We flying boatmen fly low looking for lakes and rivers on which to splash down. Splash down! What a lovely phrase, reminiscent of childhood. How thrilling the great bow-wave, roaring past the portholes as we splashed down or took off! How fascinating to meet the watermen of all shapes and colours who dashed, dived and swam out to meet you! To alight in extinct volcanoes, on sacred lakes, and swirling rivers that reminded you that this huge airborne creature was also a boat, straining at its cables. 'Bring back the flying boats!' is my cry. Splash down to Adventure!

I devoured my itinerary and smacked my lips. We would be leaving from Southampton, putting down (weather permitting) on the River Saône where it joins the Rhône in Central France; at Marignane, Marseille, where one of my great heroes, Saint-Exupéry, spent so much of his short life; on Lake Bracciano in Fascist-dominated Rome; at Alexandria; on the Sea of Galilee; at Lake Habbaniya, an RAF station in Iraq; at Sharjah on the Persian Gulf; in Baluchistan; on private lakes as we crossed India, by gracious permission of native princes and rajas; on the Jumna, on the Hooghly, on the Irrawaddy (monsoon permitting) — and all of these romantic and beautiful spots were subject to change without notice. It was pure Jules Verne, and I was living it.

JULY 11, 1937
TIBERIAS, PALESTINE
POWELL TO CUNYNGHAME,
LONDON FILMS
SPLASHED DOWN SEA OF
GALILEE. NOBODY FISHING.
MICKY

It seemed an enormity to be taxiing and gathering speed on the Sea of Galilee.

We flew on over the desert, crossing the gorges of the Euphrates and turned south to Basra. Whitey (one of a bunch of American oil engineers) sat beside me and talked about the Persian Gulf. He had been here before, but the other Americans were out for the first time.

We came down on Basra long after dark, but our skipper made a perfect landing on the river, in spite of all the flares and rockets. He was a bulky, fair-moustached, indignant man, with china-blue eyes and very short shorts depending on one small button to keep them from a spectacular collapse. He walked amusingly like Charles Laughton, he had the same short swing of the arms, and he pushed his belly before him, with the same intolerant air: 'Damn you! Yes. I'm fat. And I like it! Damn you!'

He was eating a most enormous breakfast at Basra as I looked over his shoulder in awe. He absorbed five illustrated papers, grapefruit, a couple of newspapers, haddock, reports from the flight officer, bacon, sausage, and a heap of fried tomato, marmalade, toast, iced coffee and a bunch of grapes damn you.

We slept at Basra, which means I spent a wakeful night lying under the punkah with a towel over my vital organs. This keeps one's stomach happy and full of confidence in you. The heat was torrid, the hotel first-class. I heard a good deal about Sir John Ward, the British Resident, and his wife, who matched him. He seemed to be the uncrowned King of Iraq, and the hotel, which was splendid, was his latest achievement.

Empire flying boat coming in to land at Durban   IWM CH 14073

PLAYER'S CIGARETTES
S.A.B.E.N.A.: SAVOIA-MARCHETTI S. 73

At Bahrain, our next stop, Whitey and the rest of the Americans left us. They were going 'up-country', destination unrevealed. I missed them. We had been warned not to expect home comforts that night at Sharjah and Dubai, two Arab cities on the Gulf, with natural harbours scooped out of the sand by the movement of the tides. We landed inland on a lagoon, presided over by a fort.

As we circled around, we saw the westward-bound flying boat ready to take off from the lagoon.

JULY 13, 1937
SHARJAH EMIRATE
POWELL TO KORDA
COULD YOU IMAGINE WHOLE PERSIAN GULF TO CHOOSE FROM
COLLIDED SHARJAH WITH WESTBOUND FLYING BOAT. AWAITING
REPLACEMENT FROM KARACHI.
MICKY

On our way again we stopped for fuel at Juinli. It was like a scene from the Arabian Nights. The sea was a violet indigo, there was a great bare beach, and the altogether uninhabitable interior was altogether uninhabited. It was a new fuelling post – the old one was at Gwadar – and both of them were on the marshy coast of Baluchistan. The whole coast there was a chain of salt lakes with a sand bar between them and the Indian Ocean, which came roaring in, in splendid long surf-rollers. The post had been established only two weeks previously and was pretty crude. Two engineers, who expected to be picked up by us yesterday, had had to spend the night there and were disgruntled. They were both huge young men in shorts, with enormous hairy buttocks, and they sweated absolute gulf-streams all the time and didn't speak to anyone.

Tribesmen appeared from nowhere in scarlet turbans and scanty loin-cloths and climbed on our floats. The leading Baluchi jumped into the sea with the mooring rope and swam to the mooring buoy, while his friends screamed their encouragement. When he had tied it, he climbed on top and squatted there grinning. The others flew to the job (which for them was fun, not work) of pumping petrol and pouring cans.

I sometimes think, and smile as I do so, of all the obscure corners of the world that were illuminated, held briefly in the spotlight and then allowed to lapse back into obscurity again. Lonely rivers, sacred lakes that had been left to the birds and beasts for hundreds of years, were to hear the thunder of marine engines and some native prince would dream of international airports.

Then suddenly one morning a better landing place was found, his lake was downgraded to 'Emergency Landing Only' and the sleep of centuries resumed.

We splashed down across India from Karachi to Calcutta, sometimes flying several thousands of feet up, sometimes at nought feet, below the clouds, stampeding buffalo, with villagers shaking their fists at us. Our first stop was at Udaipur, on a sacred lake full of crocodiles that we fed with ham sandwiches. All around were little hills, each one crowned with a shrine. On the biggest hill was the white fortress palace of the raja. The town of Udaipur was about 12 miles away and we saw it from the air. The reigning raja was air-minded and planned to spend four lakhs of rupees on developing an airfield. Meanwhile, he let Imperial Airways use his lake, although littering and swimming were forbidden. The last prohibition was hardly necessary after one look at the crocodiles.

We refuelled at Shaipur, a town of white marble and at Gwalior, where the citadel, its cliffs several hundred feet high, dwarfed everything else. At Allahabad we landed on the Jumna, sending ripples over the pilgrims washing their sins away in the sacred river. Calcutta, next stop! We climbed above the monsoon ceiling to 15,000 feet. Just imagine! Three miles high in a boat. How Jules Verne would have revelled in it!

A Life in Movies, Michael Powell, 1986

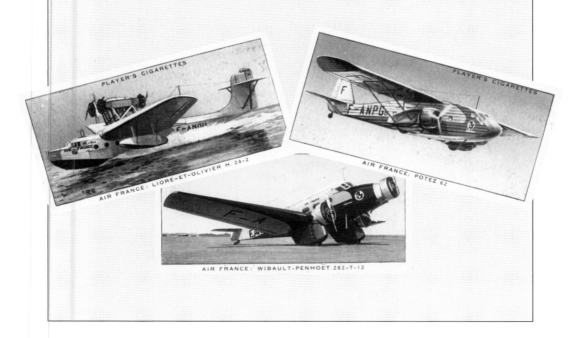

ROUTES

England – Palestine – 'Iraq –
Persia – India
England – Egypt – East Africa –
South Africa

LONDON (Croydon)
Paris
Brindisi
ATHENS
Castelrosso
Mirabella
Cyprus
Galilee
Baghdad
Alexandria
Rutbah Wells
Basra
Cairo
Bushire
Assiut
Lingeh
Aswan
Jask
Gwadar
Karachi
Wadi Halfa
INDIA
Bombay
Atbara
Khartoum
Aden
Kosti
Malakal
CEYLON
Colombo
Juba
Kampala
Lake Victoria
Kisumu
Nairobi
Moshi
Dodoma
Mbeya
Mpika
Lake Nyasa
Broken Hill
Salisbury
Bulawayo
Pietersburg
Madagascar
Johannesburg
Kimberley
Durban
Victoria West
Beaufort West
CAPE TOWN

AFRICA

N
W   E
S

Route to Palestine, 'Iraq,
Persia, India:
Route to Egypt, East Africa
and South Africa

'And I finally concluded
that if I did not fly thither
it was impossible to make
the journey'

The Travels and Adventures of Pero Tafur
1435-39

HILARY WATSON
TRAFFIC OFFICER, STEWARD AND STATION MANAGER

Though he is now physically very frail, Hilary Watson's mind is as sharp as ever. A raconteur whose description of events and characters from long ago veers entertainingly from the comic to the sublime, Hilary lives in a beautiful Regency villa in South London whose walls bear witness to his great loves: early furniture, pictures and music.

Hilary decided he was going to fly on the day he saw Zeppelins picked out by searchlights in the dark London sky during the Great War. He was born in 1910 in Stoke-on-Trent, into an Army family that travelled almost continually.

'I was a little boy staying in London with relatives,' he explains, 'and when I saw the Zeppelins I thought that if those things could fly then people would soon be able to fly easily and travel all over. It sort of registered on my mind because even at that early age I knew I was determined to see the world. But having watched the Zeppelins for a minute or two we were made to go into a cupboard under the stairs because people were terrified of the things.'

With the war over Hilary was able to travel by boat to America to visit relatives and it was there that he had his first real taste of flying.

'We went to a place where you could pay for a kind of joyride and I went up in a tiny tri-motor aeroplane. It had a sort of corrugated metal skin, and the flight was both terrifying and exhilarating. At this time I was also reading books by Jules Verne and the whole idea of travel was growing in my mind. I read everything I could lay my hands on about flying, never really thinking I'd be able to do it.

'Then, having left school and done a few uninteresting jobs, I found myself one day at Victoria Station looking at a poster put up by Imperial Airways. I must have been nineteen or twenty at the time and while I was staring at it a man came up to me and asked me if I was interested in aviation. I can still remember his name – he was Air Commodore Fletcher, the Ground Service Manager for Imperial Airways, whose offices at that time were near Victoria Station. He said if I went to his office he would give me some literature about working for Imperial Airways. I immediately thought – this is it! Anyway, we wandered off together and I noticed that as we went into his office everyone saluted him – it was all very crisp and military in those days. He was terribly kind to me and gave me maps of the routes Imperial Airways already flew as well as a big fold-out diagram of a De Havilland 42.'

Nothing came of that first meeting but Hilary had made up his mind to keep in touch with Air Commodore Fletcher.

'It was almost as if I sensed his routine and I made it my business to bump into him in and around Victoria Station. This was easy for me as I was staying with relatives nearby. He always walked through the station at the same time each day and took the same route, and I knew if I bumped into him often enough he'd offer me a job!'

Hilary's instinct was right and after numerous 'chance' meetings the two became almost friends. They spoke to each other when they met and then one day – out of the blue – it happened.

'We were chatting about nothing in particular when Air Commodore Fletcher just turned round and said, "Why don't you come and join Imperial Airways?" He told me the airline was expanding rapidly and they needed lots of young, hard-working, enthusiastic people. He said they needed people to go overseas and help set up stations. I asked him what qualifications were needed and he replied, "Common sense and hard work!" Well, that suited me right down to the ground. He took me on straight away.'

In 1934, when Hilary joined Imperial Airways, passengers began their journeys at Airways Mansions just off the Haymarket in central London. They gathered here and were taken by coach to Croydon Aerodrome. Hilary was sent to Croydon initially and his first job – 'not the most enthralling in the world!' he now says – was cleaning out the big thermos flasks that were used to take soup onto the planes. He has a wonderfully detailed memory of what was then a remarkably small-scale operation.

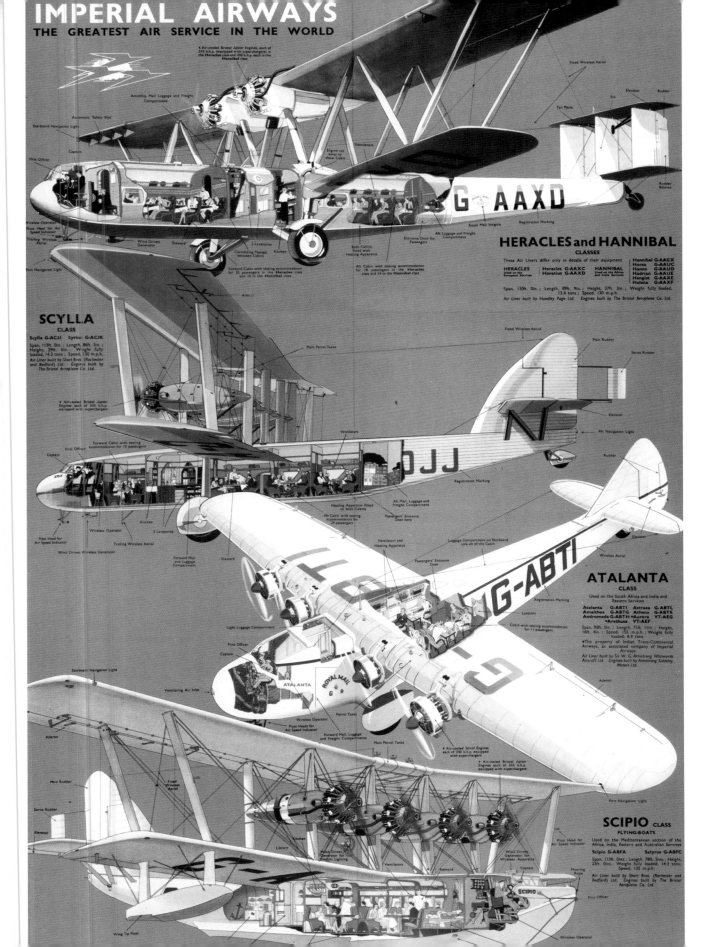

IMPERIAL AIRWAYS

EMPIRE TIME TABLE
1932
1ST EDITION

PALESTINE
'IRAQ
PERSIA
INDIA
EGYPT
ANGLO-EGYPTIAN
SUDAN

UGANDA
KENYA COLONY
TANGANYIKA
TERRITORY
RHODESIA
UNION OF
SOUTH AFRICA

PASSENGER FARES

LONDON—FRANCE, ITALY, GREECE, PALESTINE, 'IRAQ, PERSIA, AND INDIA

Quoted in £ sterling and inclusive of all accommodation, meals, and tips en route. As these fares include a proportion of expenditure in foreign currency they are liable to fluctuation without notice in accordance with the prevailing exchange rates

A link service between India and Africa is provided via Cairo

For fares from Cairo to stations on the Africa route and between Europe and Egypt by the direct service see page 7

RETURN FARES
are double the single fares less 10 cent of the total

	London	Paris	Brindisi	Athens	Castelrosso	Galilee	Baghdad	Basra	Bushire	Lingeh	Ja	G
Athens	30	27	12									
Castelrosso	40	40	24	12								
Galilee	47	47	34	24	12							
Baghdad	62	62	48	36	24	20						
Basra	67	67	53	41	29	25	6					
Bushire	72	72	58	46	34	30	11	6				
Lingeh	78	78	64	52	40	36	17	12	6			
Jask	84	84	70	58	46	42	23	18	12	6		
Gwadar	90	90	76	64	52	48	29	24	18	12		
Karachi	95	95	81	69	57	53	34	29	23	17		

CAIRO—GALILEE, £5

Note t

On arriv
morning, y
another
in which y
for your j
You are, the
it is advi
personal ca
which you ma

IMPERIAL AIRWAYS.

Station: Khartoum

Arrangements for: NORTHBOUND AIRCRAFT
You will be called at 04.30 hours and your bagg
outside your room at 04.50 hours.
Breakfast will be served at 05.00 hours.
Currency Coupons will be cashed at the rate of

The car will leave this hotel at 05.30 hours.
will leave the airport at 05.45 hours tomorrow an
be made at: Shereik, WadiHalfa and Luxor (Night s

Meals on tomorrow's journey will be served as show
Breakfast: Khartoum   Tea: Luxo
Lunch: WadiHalfa   Dinner: do.

Mr W.H. Whelan, the Company's representative, will gi
you any further information or assistance you may ne
your stay at this station.

48

Mr. Gamle

IMPERIAL AIRWAYS

Station Juba departure northboun
ARRANGEMENTS FOR 5.45   and your baggage should
You will be called at 6.15   breakfast will be served 6.15   at   6
your room at 6.15
Currency Coupons will be cashed at 240 m/m
The car will leave the hotel
The air-liner will leave the airport at 7.00   hours to-mo
will be made at Malakal Rosti Kha
Meals on to-morrow's journey will be served as shown.
BREAKFAST Juba   TEA Kharto
LUNCH in aircraft   DINNER Khart
            Bussens
Mr   the Company's representativ
any further information or assistance you may need during your stay at th

IMPERIAL AIRWAYS

LIMITED
HELIOPOLIS AERODROME,
HELIOPOLIS,
EGYPT.

Telephone: 62293/4/5

xxxxxxxxxxxxx

Codes:
BENTLEY'S
Telegram
AIRWAYS

Passengers for Greece, Italy,
France and England.
- --------------------------

CAIRO :   Monday, 1st October, 1934.

Lunch will be served in the Heliopolis
House Hotel at 1300 hours.

Currency Coupons will be cashed by the
Hall Porter at the rate of P.T.24 each.

The passenger car will leave the Hotel
at 14.15 hours for the aerodrome. The
aircraft will leave at 1430 hours
Alexandria where the night will be

The Company's representative, Mr.
will be present at the Hotel to gi
any further information or assist
require during your stay at this

---o0o---

Imperial Airwys
Northbound passengers
----

in Cairo tomorrow
will transfer to
raft similar to that
are now travelling
rney to Alexandria.
efore, reminded that
le to keep in your
any small articles
possibly mislay.

From Luxor Office

Imperial
Airways

AND INDIAN TRANS-CONTINENTAL AIRWAYS

INDIA
and Eastern Services

127

IMPERIAL AIRWAYS Ltd.

Station **Alexandria**   Date **1.10.34**

Name **GAMLEN**

1. *Passengers will be called at* **4.45** *a.m. and
   their baggage should be outside their rooms
   by* **5.15**
2. *Tea & biscuits will be at* **5.15** *a.m.*
3. *Passenger cars will leave this Hotel at* **5.45 sharp**
   the aircraft will leave the aerodrome at **06.00**
4. *Currency Coupons will be cashed at the rate
   of* **P 97 for 4**

*The Stations at which the aircraft will call to-
morrow are:-*

> **Mirabella**
> **Athens**
> **Brindisi**
> **in the train** *(Night-stop)*

Tomorrow lunch will be served
        at **on board**
    Tea at **on board**
Dinner at **in the train**

Mr **T. Munro**, *Station Superintendent,
is at your disposal to ensure your comfort whilst
staying at this port.*

IMPERIAL AIRWAYS

Station **Luxor**

ARRANGEMENTS FOR **Monday 1st October 1934**

You will be called at **06:15**
our room at **06:45**

Breakfast will be served **06:45**
and your baggage should be outside

ency Coupons will be cashed at **24.25**
will leave **the hotel**
ner will leave the airport at **08:00**
de at **Cairo, Alexandria**

at .... hours to-morrow and stops

morrow's journey will be served as shown.
in Luxor
in Cairo   TEA **in Alexandria**
S. Zammit   DINNER **in Alexandria**
ation or assistance you may need   the Company's representative, will give to you
during your stay at this station

outside

45
ow and stops
toum

um
um

will give to you
station

119

'Croydon then was tiny — there was a small kitchen where I worked and it was run by a woman whose claim to fame was that she had been the housekeeper at Claridges. There was a little stove on which she used to heat the soup to go in those flasks I spent my days cleaning. The planes used were HP42s and they flew to Paris in the main, although they could already go on from there on other flights to distant lands.

'When the passengers reached Paris they were always met by an Imperial Airways representative who took them to their hotel. When the Empire routes had been established to India, Australia and South Africa the rep took them to the train station the next morning for the train jour-ney on to Milan. Here another rep met them and they were taken to a hotel for something to eat before continuing on their rail journey to Brindisi at the foot of Italy, where they were met by yet another rep. The reason they did this bit of the journey by rail was that the planes weren't powerful enough or sophisticated enough to fly over the Swiss Alps. Within a few years I had been promoted from flask cleaner and was one of these representatives.'

Before becoming a rep, or traffic officer as they were officially known, Hilary was sent to Paris on an HP42 just to see if he could cope with it. His bosses were particularly concerned to see whether staff were prone to air-sickness, a major problem on early passenger planes which regularly hit bad weather and were unable to fly above it. 'We didn't have sick bags in those days,' remembers Hilary, 'but a sort of pot was provided under every seat.'

From 1935 Hilary was a traffic officer based in Brindisi with a small group of Imperial Airways staff. The job was simple enough — meet the passengers and look after them. They arrived by train from Milan in the morning just in time for breakfast at the Hotel International. After breakfast they were taken — by Hilary — to a Kent class flying boat for the next leg of the journey. Three of these flying boats were based at Brindisi: *Scipio*, *Sylvanus* and *Satyrus*. They ran a shuttle over the Mediterranean to Alexandria, stopping at Athens and

Travel comfortably **IMPERIAL AIRWAYS** AND ASSOCIATED COMPANIES

Europe—Africa—India—China—Australia

121

BY AIR to South Africa
or
India in less than a week!

Promenade saloon of the Empire flying-boat

IMPERIAL

AIRWAYS

Imperial Airways Ltd., Airway Terminus, SW1 ; Airways House, Charles Street, SW1. VICtoria 2211 (Day and Night), or travel agents. Imperial Airways is agent in Great Britain for Belgian Air Lines, German Airways, Swissair and Railway Air Services

HILARY WATSON

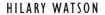

122

Crete on the way. In Crete, Imperial Airways had moored a yacht – this was the refuelling base for the flying boats.

'The Kent class flying boat carried I think about twelve passengers, and a lot at that time were big game hunters on their way to East Africa. When they got to Alexandria they transferred to a land-plane and went on to Luxor and then Kenya, so private individuals were flying in these early days but only if they were fabulously wealthy. Passengers not going on to East Africa went the other way, as it were, to Gaza, Baghdad, Basra and so on to Karachi. Traffic control officers had to wear a smart blue uniform with a cap bearing an Imperial Airways badge.'

The maximum number of passengers the HP42 could carry was twenty, and when people said that planes would soon carry thirty or more even the Imperial Airways staff thought they were mad. After a few months at Brindisi Hilary was moved to Athens and then to Alexandria.

'Generally speaking it has to be said that the passengers were so rich that they hadn't a clue how to do anything for themselves – we used to say they needed to have their noses wiped. And they were not always that well-behaved – often the first question I was asked by a new arrival in Brindisi or Athens was, "Where are the brothels?"'

By 1935–6 Imperial Airways was expanding rapidly – so rapidly in fact that it sometimes found it difficult to find enough crew to run existing services. It was at about this time that Hilary was offered a job as a steward on the HP42s shuttling between Luxor, Khartoum and Cairo.

'I was based at Cairo where we Imperial Airways staff lived in a big villa – conditions were basic but I was travelling, I was in an exotic country and it was wonderful. I think I was paid about 20 Egyptian pounds a month.

'The job was pretty straightforward – I checked all the mail before it was put on the plane, and any precious cargo, and then when we were in the air I handed out drinks to the passengers. There were no meals, but the drinks were absolutely essential as there was no air conditioning and of course it was always terribly hot. The only ventilation we had were a few little grilles open to the air on the top of the cabin.'

In 1936 Hilary's contract expired and he was sent back to England, but he had developed a passion for airline work and had no intention of trying anything else.

'I went to see my old friend Air Commodore Fletcher, who said he was delighted to see me. That made me think they might keep me on – and they did.

'Fletcher offered to let me go on leave but I loved hard work, so I said, bugger the leave – can I have another job. I think he was rather pleased at that and he told me that Imperial Airways were planning to open the first British commercial route into the USA – in fact, we wanted to be the first foreign airline to fly into the USA.

STATION MANAGER

123

'We were to be based at Bermuda which of course was a British territory. I was told that a flying boat was on its way there so that regular flights could begin from the island to the American mainland. What they didn't tell me was that the flying boat – the *Cavalier* – was on its way in crates on board the *Loch Kearn*.

'Anyway, Fletcher then said, "I'd like you to go out to Bermuda to work with the station manager." A company had been formed called Airways Bermuda Ltd and I was to be one of its first employees. I was told I had to leave in a week but I thought that was marvellous, even though I hadn't a clue where Bermuda was!'

Hilary spent a week going to the theatre in London and generally enjoying himself, and then sailed on the *Rainier del Pacifico* from Liverpool. When he arrived in Bermuda *Cavalier* had arrived and been unloaded at the Royal Naval Dockyard at the western end of the island.

'My job was really only the station manager's dogsbody, but Bermuda was a revelation – such a lovely island. I later had a narrow escape when *Cavalier* crashed – I could easily have been on board, but other than that I had a marvellous time on the island. But in those first few weeks and months we set up the station. We reached an agreement with Pan Am that they would fly

Captain H.W.C. Alger signals 'Cast away' to a launch alongside *Canopus* at a refuelling halt on the African route.

IWM CH 14060

HILARY WATSON

124

twice a week to Bermuda and back and we would fly twice a week to New York and back.

'My boss Stuart Shaw was an interesting chap but he had no experience of air passenger travel at all. In fact he was a chemist from Croydon! But then none of us, I suppose, had much experience of managing a flying boat station. We just got on with it and learned as we went. The Americans were more experienced, but I can remember the excitement as we watched *Cavalier* on its test flights with the launch steaming alongside. Bermuda was not the playground of the rich, but of the incredibly rich. Here the Vanderbilts and Rockefellers had their palaces where they escaped the worst of the New York City winters. When *Cavalier* made its first landing loaded with American passengers I rang a bell and hoisted the Union Jack.

'I was in charge of the office at Daryl's Island where we were based, but we also set up an office in the Prince's Hotel in the Bermudan capital Hamilton. The office was invaded every night by giant cockroaches and we used a special steam insecticide to kill them. It was set on a timer to go off at midnight when we'd all long gone and then in the morning we'd sweep up the victims.

'I received four planes a week – our two and the American two. We had a big, very smart launch to take the passengers to and from the flying boats – that is, from Hamilton to Daryl's Island – and the locals always gathered in groups and cheered when we brought the passengers ashore or when the planes took off or landed. We flew Gertrude Lawrence and David Astor, among a host of rich and famous people.

Passengers disembark from Boeing flying boat *Bangor* after a transatlantic flight to the UK.
IWM CH 13938

'It was a wonderful life because I became so friendly with the Americans and though our quarters on Daryl's Island were not luxurious I dined out almost every evening with these glamorous people from the East Coast.'

Hilary stayed in Bermuda without ever returning home from 1935 until the early part of World War II. But with America officially a neutral country, things then began to take a sinister turn.

'I remember the day war broke out the Clipper' (one of the big Boeing flying boats BOAC had bought from Pan-Am) 'was due in from Lisbon carrying refugees – when it arrived it was filled with all sorts of European royalty including the last Empress of Austria.

'The war period was strange in lots of ways. Because America was neutral early on in the war all mail from occupied Europe coming into Bermuda to go on to America had to be censored. Then, for reasons that I still don't fully understand to this day, I was asked to leave the island at very short notice. I'd always loved German opera, particularly Wagner, and was sometimes nicknamed Fritz because of this – so that may have had something to do with it. Perhaps they thought I was a spy or something! But whatever it was I was having dinner one night with some friends when a policeman I knew well came into the restaurant and said he wanted to see me. He served me with a deportation order to leave within three days. He said he couldn't tell me why, but I didn't mind much as I wanted to return anyway and do my bit for the war effort.

'I flew to New York and went to see Uncle Paul – Imperial Airways' man in our offices in the Empire State Building. He booked me on a ship and a few

Travelling to the USA on war service in the cabin of BOAC flying boat *Berwick*. All decorations and luxury fittings were removed for the duration.   IWM CH 14041

HILARY WATSON

126

weeks later I was back in England, only to discover that London had almost shut down and BOAC – which is what Imperial Airways had become in 1940 – had decamped to Bristol.

'I was the only passenger on that ship to England and we didn't join a convoy – safety in numbers and all that – until two days later. It took three weeks to get to Liverpool because we went up and down, left and right, crisscrossing back and forth to avoid submarines.

'I remember coming up the Mersey and seeing the barrage balloons – it was 1942, probably the darkest year of the war. I was told to report to BOAC's HQ in Bristol where they were enjoying life at the Grand Spa Hotel. I was told I'd done a good job in Bermuda and then sent off for a week's holiday, which I spent in London listening to concerts and visiting the few theatres still open. I particularly enjoyed the lunchtime concerts given by Myra Hess at St Martin-in-the-Fields. Back in Bristol a week later I was told to go to Dublin the following Monday, where I was to run a secret flying boat base at Foynes on the River Shannon. This was the nearest place to the USA where the Boeing 314 flying boats could land. The loads – passengers and freight – the flying boats were to carry were assembled at Whitchurch in the West Country and then flown to Ireland by land-plane. Freight and passengers were then driven to the flying boats for the onward journey to the USA, or to Lisbon and then West Africa to feed and supply Britain's North African army.

'When I discovered that I was supposed to run the whole operation at Foynes together with a chap called Tom Monroe, I thought, "This will be a hell of a job." I was flown over in a blacked-out plane and met by an Aer Lingus rep who escorted me to the train for Limerick. I remember that because there was no coal the train had to stop regularly to pick up turf – huge piles of the stuff were stacked at intervals by the side of the track and we all had to get off to help load it!'

Foynes had been a small coastal coaling and fishing village, but all the trade had gone and the new flying boat station was welcomed by the locals because it brought badly needed employment.

Hilary was now officially a senior traffic officer but still organizing passengers and freight as he'd done in Bermuda, although of course now instead of rich East Coast Americans he was dealing almost entirely with military personnel – 'but we also carried Anthony Eden and there was still an occasional member of an obscure European Royal family.

'The thing about the airline world at that time was that everyone knew everyone else – it was a very small world and even now I keep in touch with several people – also in their nineties – from those days.

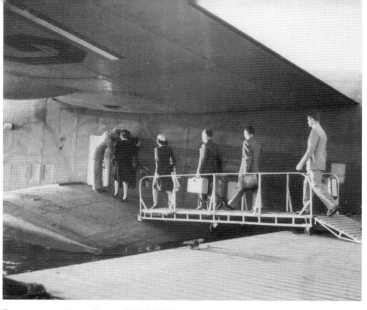

Passengers boarding a BOAC Boeing flying boat at Baltimore prior to taking off for the transatlantic flight to Britain.
IWM CH 15308

'At Foynes we used to say that the Irish were neutral in the war, but neutral in our favour – in fact working in Ireland was a delight. Everyone was so helpful. I stayed for four years in the end and lived off the fat of the land. I was always sending food to friends in England. The only difficulties the job involved were caused by having to work with Americans – the customs work was complicated and we were badgered continually by every ministry for seats on planes. There were never enough to go round and all sorts of special pleading went on. If we hadn't been able to juggle claims the planes would have been too heavy to take off!

'There was also the problem that everything was so hush-hush that I had to use a code for all communications – I kept forgetting the code so I kept it on a bit of string round my neck! I also had the only private telephone line directly from Ireland to England – I used to keep the phone under my bed!

'Foynes closed towards the end of the war, my boss was made redundant and I began to worry about what I was going to do. I was called to our head office in Ireland and then sent back to Bristol. Then, despite my worries about redundancy, I was sent to Gibraltar where I worked with several old colleagues and friends.'

Hilary stayed in Gibraltar for two years and was then sent as a senior traffic officer to Poole in Dorset. He was based at both Hurn, now Bournemouth Airport, and Poole, so he shuttled between the two. Hurn was used by land-planes, Poole by flying boats.

'I did this for a while,' he explains, 'but my love of travel had never left me

and I wanted to see South America. I was fascinated by what I'd read about Inca and Mayan culture and then I heard that Air Vice Marshall Don Bennett, who ran the Pathfinders in Bomber Command, had formed an airline called British South American Airways. The war had only just ended and I thought I'd try to get a job with this new airline. I knew I'd get no higher at BOAC – we all suspected that old Imperial Airways people were not looked on favourably by the management. I had the sort of experience BSAA were looking for and I got a job as traffic supervisor to run the Lisbon–Dakar–Rio line. We also went to Montevideo and eventually to Peru. I engaged all the staff we needed and flew between the various stations to check that everything was as it should be. I was based in Piccadilly in central London but went out regularly to South America, and of course I got to see all those wonderful Inca and Mayan sites I'd read about.

'I started with BSAA in the early 1950s, grew to hate all the office politics associated with the job and was eventually tempted away by an offer of a job with the Northern Transport Agency, organizing flying tours of America for the Royal Shakespeare Company and other theatre businesses trying to break into the American market. I was released by BSAA for two years but with the knowledge that I could go back if things didn't work out. For various reasons they didn't, so I returned to BSAA. By this time BSAA had been taken over by BOAC anyway, and while wondering what I should do next I met the chairman of the Decca Recording Company at a party and we discussed opera, which was the great love of my life. I think he must have been impressed because shortly afterwards he offered me a job in the Decca export department. He needed someone who knew about music but was also well travelled, so I suppose I fitted the bill perfectly. So having spent nearly twenty years working in the airline business I found myself in the record business. I became export manager and then director, and met all the stars I'd once dreamed about, from Joan Sutherland to Pavarotti. I finally retired in 1976.

'Two highlights of my flying days: I once pulled Simon Marks of Marks & Spencer fame from a crashed Frobisher in Ireland. Along with the other passengers he was, I'm glad to say, completely uninjured. On another occasion I heard the phone ring under my bed while I was in Ireland. It was Winston Churchill, and despite the fact that he was the Prime Minister I had to ask him to hold because I had a call on another line!'

HILARY WATSON

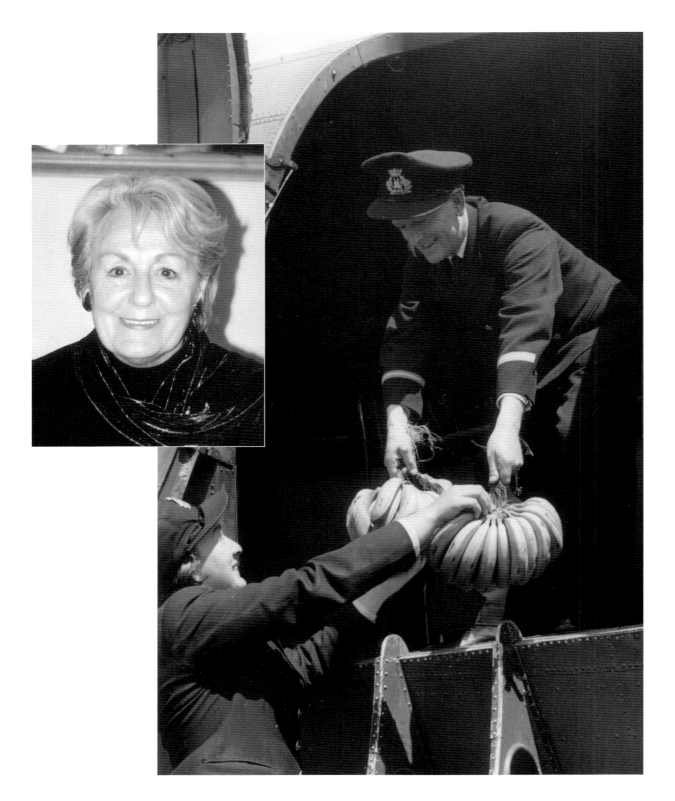

HAZEL ROSE
STEWARDESS

Hazel Rose was an air stewardess in the days when stewardesses were almost invariably very well-connected girls who'd been to expensive private schools. Working on the new passenger services was seen as an acceptable employment for well-bred girls – but only so long as they did not marry. Hazel was born in 1932 in the tiny Yorkshire village of Hooton Roberts between Sheffield and Doncaster and she is the first to admit that, on the face of it, she did not fit the stereotypical stewardess image. For a start her parents were not well-off.

'The truth is they just couldn't keep me on at school,' she says with a broad smile. 'They would have but they didn't have the money.'

From early childhood, however, Hazel had two driving ambitions – to be a nurse and to travel, and she was determined to do both.

'I went to nursing college but it was a long way from the little village where I lived with my parents. In fact it was a one and a half hour journey each way and no buses even if you felt you could put up with it.'

Then along came what looked like a solution – Hazel got the chance to go and live with a friend's aunt and uncle in Bournemouth, on the South Coast, where she still lives today.

'It was a wonderful opportunity because Bournemouth was a big town even then and I knew there would be a hospital nearby where I might be able to get a place to train as a nurse.'

As it turned out her nursing career was not to be, but she flourished in the busy South Coast town.

Punch, September 7 1955

B.O.A.C. takes good care of you — personally!

The Captain of the aircraft is a real, dedicated airman, with thousands and thousands of flying hours . . . but still time for the youngest of travellers. He likes to chat to his passengers — the passengers like it, too.

The friendly, courteous attention of skilled B.O.A.C. aircrews — always competent, never obtrusive — ensures that you'll enjoy every moment of your B.O.A.C. flight.

Consult your local Travel Agent or any B.O.A.C. office.

FLY ➤ B·O·A·C

BRITISH OVERSEAS AIRWAYS CORPORATION

'I loved it, and although the local hospital had no vacancies I wasn't too bothered because I got a job in a hotel and my experience there was to stand me in good stead for my later time as a stewardess.'

Hazel worked in several hotels in Bournemouth and had different jobs so she got to know how hotels were run. Then when she was nineteen she thought she'd better get the travel bug out of her system so with a Danish girlfriend she decided to go hitch-hiking in France, which was almost unheard-of in 1953.

'It was a wonderful adventure. We didn't have any money — I think I had about £8 to last three months! We went from Southampton to Cherbourg up through France to Switzerland then via Provence and Marseille to Italy. We stayed in youth hostels and travelled in the backs of lorries — we were told that as we were girls it was OK to get lifts as long as we didn't get into the lorry cab!

'I mention all this because travelling like this got me interested in languages and I started to learn French. It also made me more street-wise, which I think helped enormously when I got my first job on a passenger plane.

'Anyway, after three months I was dropped by Danish friends at Dunkirk and had to borrow the money from the local police to pay my ferry fare home!'

It was soon after this that Hazel met her husband-to-be, who was already working for BOAC as a steward. He'd just returned from South Africa.

'He was looking wonderfully handsome and tanned and I suppose that talking to him when we first met made me realize that there was a way to travel and get paid for it. This would have been 1954.

'As my boyfriend was working for BOAC I thought, well, why don't I try,

132

All over the world B.O.A.C. takes good care of you

although I knew it would be difficult because it was common knowledge that stewardesses were always wealthy and very well educated.'

Hazel knew all this by hearsay before she joined BOAC but if she had any doubts they were quickly dispelled when she did finally join, for the girls who later became her friends had fathers who were High Court judges or surgeons

Hazel Rose photographed soon after successfully completing her training at BOAC.

or owned huge companies. The girls themselves seemed to have almost limitless finances.

'They probably didn't need to work for the money anyway,' explains Hazel, 'but flying was glamorous and rather chic, I suppose, which is what appealed to them. And flying must have seemed a very attractive alternative to the sort of jobs girls usually ended up with, like secretarial work.

'So when I applied I really didn't think I'd get in – I had a Yorkshire accent, I hadn't been to an expensive private school and I was too short. For safety reasons the airlines had a rule that girls who wanted to be stewardesses had to be at least 5 foot 4 inches tall and I was at least a couple of inches below that. I got round that problem eventually by getting specially made shoes that looked like the uniform shoes but had a heel. You needed the height just to reach the overhead lockers!

'While I was still thinking of applying to BOAC I got myself a job as an au pair for a while in France – it was a chance for me to practise my French which was something I knew I would need if I was ever to get a job as a stewardess. I worked for a judge's daughter who had one child. I didn't learn much but I had a wonderful time! I'd actually applied to BOAC just before I left England. The girl I'd been staying with in Bournemouth eventually sent the reply from BOAC on to me in France. I came back in September 1956 and set off for Heathrow for my interview.

'I had to borrow a smart suit and white shirt from a girlfriend and then – disaster! While I was on the train I spilled coffee all down my nice shirt. It looked like fate was trying to make sure I didn't get the job! When I got to the station in London I rushed out and bought a new shirt and got to the interview just in time.

'Lots of girls were milling around in the waiting area outside the room where, one by one, we went in to be interviewed by the panel. In those days it was a panel of seven and they really grilled you. As I sat outside with the other girls I realized that all I'd heard about how aristocratic they were likely to be was true. I was the only one who didn't sound upper-class and when I was called in I walked through the door, tripped and fell over! Not a good start. I was on my knees looking up into seven pairs of eyes. So I thought it would be best if I started again. I stood up, walked out, closed the door and then went back in as if nothing had happened.

'Later on I got to know one or two of the panel quite well – but on that first day it was really quite intimidating. They asked me all sorts of questions such as how I would deal with a child who needed a tourniquet, or what I would do if there was an emergency and I had to help people off the aeroplane. I thought it was all just common sense, but when I talked to the other girls afterwards I realized that they'd found a lot of the practical questions really difficult because they'd led such sheltered lives. They'd never done anything on their own or had any practical experi-

Women teleprinter operators at work at Whitchurch airport during the war.

IWM CH 14326

ence dealing with people. They knew nothing about preparing and serving food either, whereas I'd worked in various hotels dealing with people with all sorts of problems and complaints. I think that gave me an advantage over the others. I was a bit stuck when they asked me to say 30,000 in French – my mind just went blank; and I answered some other questions in French by using English words wherever I couldn't remember the French word so it must have sounded pretty odd!

'Right through the interview – which was a bit like University Challenge but in this case one person had to answer all the questions – one man on the panel said absolutely nothing. He just stared at me. Eventually, for some reason which I still can't work out, I winked at him! All the other girls were really embarrassed by him but I don't remember being afraid or worried at all – it was just that although I was young I'd done different jobs and was used to all sorts of people. When we got to the catering questions I was fine, but of course commercial catering wasn't something they taught you at finishing school.

'They asked would I mind being away for several weeks at a time, and when I said I wouldn't they only had to look at my papers to see that it was true because I'd spent months on the Continent already. They also liked the fact that I'd done some nursing and all these factors may have outweighed the fact that I didn't even have my school leaving certificate! However, my old headmaster had given me a glowing report, which surprised me as I was certainly no angel!

'Anyway, the interview ended and I went off with the other girls to have

a coffee and we got talking. They all said what their fathers did and then it was my turn – I said, "He's in steel," and they all immediately assumed he owned a foundry. I said, "He doesn't own it, he shovels it!" He was a furnaceman. Now you might think that they would then think I wasn't one of them but in fact that really broke the ice and we got on wonderfully. So much so that I'm still in

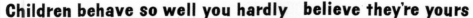

Children behave so well you hardly believe they're yours

touch with several of the girls I met that day. What really astonished me was that they all owned cars – imagine that in 1956, when there were hardly any cars around.'

Returning to Bournemouth after her interview Hazel was convinced that she would never be offered the job, but her practical experience and forthright personality clearly did the trick and she was offered a place at BOAC's training school. 'I was astonished. In fact my whole family couldn't believe it.

'The six weeks' training was at Heathrow, which was pretty much a few green fields and basic buildings in those days. We were taught what to do in a range of emergencies including ditching on water, and a range of medical procedures. We were also taught how to use lots of drugs – basic drugs that were kept in a box on every plane for emergencies. Oddly, that box could only ever be opened by the captain.'

Hazel stresses that her training was meticulous and thorough. Routines and procedures were carefully drummed into new recruits.

'They even had a mock-up of an emergency landing with the hostesses or stewardesses helping people into their life jackets and down chutes. The main thing was to stay calm whatever happened, and most of what we had to do in the mid-1950s has remained the same to this day. The real differences are that

Hazel and colleagues in the early 1950s.

HAZEL ROSE

138

the planes then were noisier and far more prone to turbulence than they are now. And of course the journeys took so much longer.

'The funniest bit of the training was when we took the dinghies down to the local swimming pool so that our instructors could check that we could turn them right side up in water!

'In fact my training stood me in good stead long after I'd stopped working for BOAC. I was once flying over Spain as a passenger when someone fainted and the air hostess went to open a portable oxygen bottle near a smoker – there could have been an explosion and I don't think the air hostess had a clue. BOAC in fact had the best trained cabin crew in the world – I think we were always the most smartly turned out, too. The uniform was a skirt and jacket in navy blue and a white blouse – very simple compared to lots of today's uniforms. And you had to wear white gloves – gloves now seem pretty much to have gone.

'We were taught how to serve the meals and how to pick up the passengers and bring them to the aircraft – sounds pretty straightforward but BOAC had a very precise idea about how they wanted it done. You had a passenger list which told you about special diets, details about VIPs if there were any, about any passengers who suffered from any illness or any who were nervous fliers.

'At the end of our six weeks' training we were given really rigorous tests which I passed easily. I think it was all down to confidence. Mind you, they did tell me my weak points – I think they thought I was rather forgetful so they told me that I should write everything down! They were right, too, because once I got the timings all wrong and served the tea over the Atlantic at three in the morning!

'A new stewardess was always given Rome as a first trip. Supervision was provided by an experienced hostess who came along just to keep an eye on things. I first flew on Constellations and after eighteen months moved to Britannias. In the two years I worked as a stewardess the Constellation was the only plane I could ever identify – it had a very distinctive tail. Passengers often asked technical questions about the planes and if they did I always went and got the engineer!

'I remember on one occasion I'd picked up my passengers and was taking them out to a Britannia when one of the passengers said to me, "That's a Britannia over there," and he was pointing in a completely different direction from the one in which I was taking them! "Only testing!"

'After my first chaperoned trip I was fine, and in fact few of us had any problems because the training was so good.

'On the Constellations we had far fewer passengers than they have on modern planes. Sometimes the whole plane was given over to first-class passengers but by today's standards all the passengers were travelling first

Passengers passing through Whitchurch airport during the Second World War.
IWM CH 14332

class – there was far more room than today and a much more personal service from the cabin crew. In the women's loo we would put out lots of very expensive cosmetics.

'A typical day would start always at Building 221 at Heathrow. We'd collect our papers – the briefing sheet – telling us all about today's passengers. With the passengers on board we did a head count so we could compare the number on board with the number of passengers actually on the pass list. We'd then report that everything had been checked and the chief steward would tell the captain and we'd be off.

'Odd things do happen on flights, too – on one occasion Duncan Sandys, the government minister, was flying with us and I saw his secretary injecting herself in the toilet. I told her to stop it immediately – I thought she was taking heroin or something! In fact she was a diabetic, but wasn't on my list of special passengers.

'Mostly I did the Far East run – to Sydney, Singapore, Tokyo, and Hong Kong which was my favourite place. But for me one of the best bits of the job was that at last I was really travelling – in those days we'd fly to Rome and stop for two days, then to Beirut where we'd get another two days, then Karachi and two days there. Today you fly to Rome and turn round and fly back – we used our two days to explore and we were paid an allowance to do it. It's only now I realize how privileged we were and how much fun we had!

'The stewardess's job has changed completely in this respect – much more pressurized and less time to enjoy anything. We didn't always stop for two days but it was never less than a day. Sometimes three to five days.

'In Beirut they put us up in the Bristol Hotel which was wonderfully luxurious – many years later, when Beirut had gone from being the Paris of the Middle East to being one of the most dangerous places in the world, I saw the hotel on TV as it was blown up, which was very sad. All I could remember when I saw that was how my girlfriends and I used to skate on the ice rink that had been built in the basement of the hotel.

'The passengers always seemed to be really nice to us too – none of that rudeness you hear about today when flying is such a pressurized business. Mind you, the other girls used to say the passengers were too scared of me to be rude! But people were more timid then, more afraid of flying – you could see it in their faces and their hands – we used to watch along the aisles for passengers whose knuckles had gone white during take-off or landing.

'I was an auntie a few times – that meant you were assigned to a child flying on his or her own. They were usually diplomats' children and horribly precocious. Mostly we sat and played cards with them, but if there were several children on board the engineers would turn the seats round so they could face each other over a table.

'I only ever had one serious incident during my flying days. We were on a Britannia and we'd taxied away from the airport buildings at Bombay and had reached the point from which we were to start our take-off run. The engines were being revved up and in the second that we moved off, the tarmac under the wheels gave way and we literally sank into the runway. That was bad enough, but of course as we went down, the propellers, which were turning at a terrific speed, smashed into the tarmac – there was mayhem, with sparks like fireworks coming off the props and deafening noise. The massive jolting threw me across the cabin, although the passengers were all strapped in so they were all right. My back still hurts from that incident, but the passengers stayed calm and our excellent training meant that we had the doors open and the chutes out in less than a minute and the passengers were soon off the plane.

'That was in 1957 and by January 1958 I was back in England and married. The rule was that married women could not work as stewardesses, but I cheated and kept quiet. That meant I was able to work for another six months. I think the authorities actually knew I was married, but I was discreet about it so they let me carry on.

'After I finished flying I did a number of different jobs, but I wouldn't have missed my flying days for the world.'

A true story about Flagship travel that might have happened to any couple

PRIORITY PASSENGER

In the early days of 1942 *Berwick* was detained at Baltimore on official instruction. The Prime Minister, Mr Winston Churchill, and the staff of his first mission to America, were at that time conferring with President Roosevelt in Washington. News of the visit faded from the newspapers, and the new battleship, HMS *Duke of York*, vanished quietly from Chesapeake Bay; it was the general guess that the Prime Minister had sailed in her. But on 12 January the Flight Captain of Boeings, Captain J. C. Kelly-Rogers, was called to the British Embassy in Washington where, under a seal of secrecy and with no names mentioned, he was told to prepare for a special flight to Bermuda. He was to be followed by two American Clippers to carry other members of a party of ninety passengers to be taken to that island.

Intricate devices were arranged to hide the fact that *Berwick* was engaged on anything unusual. All the routine of a normal Atlantic flight was undergone. The crew passed through Customs and Immigration, signals were made; but at the last moment the two pursers changed into civilian clothes and drove by car to Washington, where they boarded a special train and got to work preparing the luggage of the official party. Meanwhile Captain Kelly-Rogers, with the rest of his crew, took off from Baltimore; not till they were airborne did the captain tell the crew that they were not proceeding direct to Bermuda, but to the harbour of Norfolk, Virginia, to pick up an important load of passengers.

The two Clippers moored up at Norfolk soon after *Berwick*, and the captains held conference in the Commanding Admiral's office at the air station. It was arranged that *Berwick* would lead the formation until they were one hour out from Bermuda. Then one of the Clippers, breaking wireless silence to obtain radio bearings from a ship stationed near Bermuda for that purpose, would take the lead.

The crew slept aboard *Berwick* and rose at 4 a.m. Half an hour later, when the special train arrived from Washington, the guessed-at secret of the identity of the official party was revealed; it was, of course, the Prime Minister and members of his mission.

Mr Churchill was the last to come aboard *Berwick*, full of interest at the size and comfort of the flying boat. Soon after he was aboard she slipped the buoy and took off into a cloudless winter sky with light surface haze. She was carrying twenty-five of the party, distributed throughout her cabins. The Prime Minister was placed in the private cabin, the peacetime honeymoon suite, in the tail. He took breakfast there, though every other meal on board he took in the saloon, with the rest of the party.

Churchill at the controls of *Berwick* over the Atlantic.   IWM H 16645

After breakfast, when he had changed into his famous siren suit, the Prime Minister was conducted round the flying boat by Captain Rogers. He seemed impressed by her equipment and structure, and noted particularly the walkways inside the wings, into which an engineer can go to adjust the engines in flight. As he reached their duty stations, the members of the crew were introduced to Mr Churchill – Captain A. C. Loraine the copilot, Captain Shakespeare the chief officer, first Officer R. G. Buck the navigator, and the others. At this time *Berwick* was flying at 8000 feet through a clear blue sky above a layer of cumulus cloud.

Mr Churchill, having been assured that it was perfectly safe to smoke, lit a cigar and eagerly accepted Captain Rogers's invitation to try *Berwick*'s controls for himself. He took the captain's seat and flew her with enthusiasm for about twenty minutes, once putting her into a couple of slightly banked

turns, and commenting on the vast differences between this flying boat and the first aircraft he had flown in 1913.

They reached the point at which the American Clipper was to take the lead into Bermuda itself. Mr Churchill listened to the brief conversation between Captain Rogers and the Clipper's pilot, Lieutenant Gillespie of the United States Navy. It seemed unwise for the Prime Minister to speak to Gillespie over the radio, but he was introduced to him at Bermuda next day.

When they reached Bermuda Mr Churchill was invited to take the copilot's seat for alighting, which was made after a brief sightseeing circuit of the island on 15 January.

Captain Rogers did not know, once he had alighted at Bermuda, whether anything more would be required of him. As he was lunching in Berwick on the harbour waters, however, a launch came out with a message that he was required immediately at Government House. There he was cordially greeted by the Prime Minister who said that they were going to have a conference, with himself in the chair; the other members of the conference included Air Chief Marshal Sir Charles Portal, Admiral of the Fleet Sir Dudley Pound, the Prime Minister's Flag Commander, his secretary Mr Martin, and Captain Gordon Store of British Overseas Airways.

It was held in the drawing room of Government House, through the windows of which could be seen HMS *Duke of York* riding at anchor in the harbour.

Mr Churchill opened the conference. 'Outside lies the *Duke of York* waiting to take me to England, which I can reach in seven to nine days,' he said. 'During that time I have ears to hear but no lips with which to speak. On the other hand, Captain Kelly-Rogers assures me that in the aeroplane in which we have flown to Bermuda today we can fly to England tomorrow in not more than twenty-two hours. This is many days saved, and during that time many things may happen. Two important battles may be fought, and one major decision.' He paused, and then added, 'Such a flight cannot be regarded as a war necessity, but it is a war convenience.'

Captain Jack Kelly-Rogers.   IWM CH 13987

The conference then resolved into a stringent cross-examination of Captain Rogers on the capabilities of his flying boat, and of what his actions would be in various possible emergencies. Although naturally anxious that flight should be chosen, for the honour it would pay to the British merchant air service, the captain could not ignore the importance and responsibility of such a passenger; he tried to avoid giving the impression of seeking to influence the Prime Minister in his decision. At last Mr Churchill turned to the conference with the remark, 'He seems to have all the answers, doesn't he?' Captain Rogers said that he felt confidence in speaking as he did, simply because the merchant airmen had gained sufficient experience to regard such a flight as an everyday occurrence, a result of having all the answers. The Prime Minister decided that, should weather conditions permit a start the following morning, he would travel by air; should the forecast forbid the start that morning, he would go in the *Duke of York*.

Sir Charles Portal would act for him in all matters relating to the flight, but the final decision as to whether to proceed would be taken by Captain Rogers. The passenger list would be restricted to seven, headed by the Prime Minister himself, Sir Charles Portal, Sir Dudley Pound and Lord Beaverbrook.

It can be imagined with what feelings the captain visited the meteorological offices that day, where, under the charge of Dr Macky, the weather forecasts were being prepared. Captain Rogers admitted that he had thrown away the idea that the flight was a routine matter, finding himself with no wish to sleep, nor to eat much. He entered into calculations of fuel, deciding to take 5000 US gallons, making the all-up weight of the flying boat 87,684 lb at take-off. Similarly, each member of the crew was engaged in preparation in his own particular province.

Early next morning, 16 January, the two pilots and the navigator went to the meteorological office, where the final forecast was just being made. It showed considerable cloud over the English shore. They sent a signal to all stations concerned giving the estimated time of arrival at Pembroke Dock, in Britain, as 09.00 hours GMT next morning, with a calculated flight time of seventeen hours twenty-five minutes from take-off to touchdown.

By 10 o'clock in the morning the passengers came down to the quay, Mr Churchill sunning himself on a veranda of the airport building, waiting for take-off. By 11.36 hours *Berwick* was slipping her moorings and taxiing-out. In spite of her load, she lifted from the water only fifty-seven seconds after her throttles were opened. She climbed swiftly to 8000 feet, to gain the most of the following wind, and settled down to cruising speed, on the Crab line course from Bermuda to Pembroke Dock.

Perhaps one may be permitted a few intimate glances at this distinguished party of passengers, during the first transatlantic flight by a British Prime Minister, or for that matter by the leader of any nation. One may see them gathering at lunch in the saloon, talking of matters of State which had been concluded at Washington, the Prime Minister afterwards lighting his cigar and inviting the flying boat's captain to join them at coffee, confessing to the sense of fun with which he was enjoying his journey, and the surprise with which his colleagues in England would find him amongst them five days before he was expected; then retiring to his private cabin to sleep for a little while, afterwards to open a briefcase, summon his secretary, and get to work.

Perhaps one may even watch the Chief of the Air Staff, relaxing with his fellow travellers through the long hours of flight, confounding the first Sea Lord with a few card tricks. And if that is something of an intrusion, surely one can follow Sir Charles Portal, Lord Beaverbrook and Sir Dudley Pound onto the flight deck, displaying great interest in the working of the flying boat, and the processes of her navigation. Several times the captain was called to the private cabin where Mr Churchill was working, to report on the progress of the flight; later he issued frequent bulletins, stating the aircraft's position, speed, fuel consumption, and so on.

After dinner, when darkness had fallen, Mr Churchill and Lord Beaverbrook ascended to the flight deck, where they stood for some while gazing through the windows at the brilliantly starlit sky through which *Berwick* was riding, with stardust brushed across the carpet of cloud below. In such serenity, they told Captain Rogers that they envied him his job. Later they flew into cloud, and ice began to form on the wings. The captain focused a spotlight on the leading edge of the wing, and asked them to watch the ice being broken off as he operated the de-icer boots – a mechanism which moves the leading edge with a wriggling motion, splitting away the ice.

Until darkness fell, and they could take a sight of the stars, the crew did not know how fast they had been travelling, for they were deliberately keeping wireless silence. They knew by the sun that they were on track, but the first star fix showed them to be 90 miles ahead of the flight plan, having averaged 199 miles an hour since take-

One of BOAC's three Boeing flying boats. IWM

off, and reached a speed of 207 miles during the last hour. The engines were running sweetly, with the carburettors on hot air for a great deal of the journey, and they flew through ice every time they touched rain or cloud.

In his own mind the captain was checking off, as they passed them, the various milestones in any long-distance ocean flight – the point of three-engine non-return, the point of four-engine non-return, the points at which various alternative alighting places such as the Azores or Gibraltar were eliminated from his plans (he always had enough fuel to alight at any alternative place in the British Isles).

Towards dawn, when Mr Churchill was dressing after a good sleep in his cabin, and putting on the shoes which the steward had insisted on warming to a nice temperature for him in the oven in his galley, the radio officers were gathering weather reports from Britain which spoke of deteriorating conditions.

At dawn, Mr Churchill came up to the flight deck to watch the sunrise over the Atlantic which seen from an aircraft is comparable to no other in the world. Beneath them the indeterminate floor of cloud tops was almost black, the sky ahead dark grey.

The captain had scant time to watch the dawn. Just as it broke he began his power descent from 10,000 feet, until fifty minutes later he was at only 1000 feet, and approaching Land's End. The sky at this time was remarkably clear, and lookouts had been quietly posted through the aircraft against the approach of enemies. Mr Churchill, indeed, did enquire casually what would be done were enemy aircraft to be sighted, but the captain practised his solitary moment of evasion, and managed to avoid without remark the one question he would rather not be asked.

In such a clear sky, he afterwards confessed, he was feeling a little too naked for comfort. But the weather soon changed to rain showers, and then fog. He had already learned that the weather at Pembroke Dock was shutting down fast, with a visibility of only 500 yards, and had adopted the suggestion to change course towards Plymouth, where the clouds covered the sky at 1000 feet, and visibility was 4 miles. Now, with fog, he asked on the radio for his first bearing, and then set course to pass just south of the Lizard. He had climbed to 1500 feet, to fly just over the top of dense fog, beneath which, he told Mr Churchill who was seated in the copilot's seat, lay the English coast.

Captain Shakespeare took that seat for the final approach, which was made on the automatic direction-finder; a few minutes later he said, 'The coast.' Looking down, Captain Rogers could see the Mewstone through the fog, then Statton Heights, then the RAF station at Mount Batten, his destination.

As he circled the Sound, he noted that the balloon barrage had been short-hauled. On his first descent he lost horizontal visibility, so he climbed and circled again; this time, with Drake's Island just visible ahead but the Hoe shrouded, he crossed the breakwater at 50 feet, throttled back and alighted. Weather conditions had certainly been deteriorating, but the captain stated they had caused him no concern whatsoever.

Thus the Prime Minister made his first Atlantic crossing, a journey of 3,365 statute miles from Bermuda to Plymouth, which had been flown in seventeen hours fifty-five minutes. The flight time had been a little faster than anticipated, but the diversion to Plymouth at the end had added something to its length. Actually, having signalled from Bermuda an estimated time of arrival of 09.00 hours GMT, *Berwick* touched down at Plymouth at 08.59 hours on 17 January, one minute ahead of schedule.

While still on board, Mr Churchill caused to be prepared a statement to the public, announcing his journey and the manner in which he had travelled, so that the world might be told he had been brought safely home by the British merchant air service. Next day Captain Rogers was invited to join a family reunion luncheon at No. 10 Downing Street, in order that Mrs Churchill might express to him her thanks for having carried her husband safely back to her.

LEN REDDINGTON
WIRELESS OPERATOR

Wireless operators were the eyes and ears of an aeroplane in the days before voice communication between ground and air was possible. As communications technology improved rapidly through the 1950s, their job – once absolutely vital to the safety of the plane – was consigned to the history books, but a few of the old highly skilled operators are still with us. Len Reddington is one. Born in the East End of London in 1921, he left school at fourteen and, never thinking he might one day fly, took a job as an outdoor clerk. This rather Dickensian role was played out in the corridors of the law.

'I was a glorified office boy with a bicycle!' he recalls. 'I worked for a firm of solicitors in the City and had to run round carrying letters and documents to Courts offices, or set off on my bicycle around London delivering summonses. They liked using a boy for this sort of work because no one worried about a small boy at the door. They'd open it without thinking, and once you'd identified the recipient you'd shove the summons in their hand and then run. If they didn't take it the summons didn't count, but once they had it they weren't very happy so you had to be quick on your feet.'

Len's working career started in 1936 and he stayed with the firm of solicitors for two years. Then in 1938 he went to work in the world's biggest cement works, at West Thurrock in Essex. Business was booming for the cement industry because so many airfields were being built, but by the time war started Len, like so many other young men, was keen to join up.

'I was keen but my employer had other ideas,' he recalls. 'My work at the

cement works was semi-reserved so it wasn't easy, but by now I was addicted to the whole idea of flying so I applied to join the Air Force. I'd been spending my weekends cycling up to a place near Stansted where Hillman Airways – Hillman as in the cars – operated services to the Continent, using De Havilland Rapide twin-engined biplanes. I used to watch their planes taking off and landing hour after hour. It was a hell of a cycle from London but worth it.'

With the war on, Len was sent by his parents to a village called Orsett, near Brentwood. This was unspoiled countryside in those days – it's since been swallowed up by London. But it meant he was much closer to his job and didn't have to cycle 17 miles each way every day. He also joined the Local Defence Volunteer scheme, later to become the Home Guard, and served with the Orsett platoon.

'When I did eventually join the Air Force they decided I was short-sighted, which was a bit of a blow. It

meant I couldn't be a pilot, but there were other jobs and I was told I'd be sent to Air Crew Reception at Cardington to see if they could make anything of me.' Cardington in Bedfordshire had previously been the base for Britain's airship industry in the 1920s and 1930s, where the ill-fated R101 was built. Its two giant airship hangars, each of which occupies 5 acres of ground, still dominate the landscape. 'I was there for five days, had all sorts of written and oral tests and passed everything except – once again – my eyesight. They said I would probably be accepted anyway and put me on what was called the defence service, which involved sending me away, but with a badge to show that I wasn't a shirker! Three months later they decided my eyesight was not so bad after all and accepted me on condition I wore spectacles.

'My final call-up was a long time coming, despite all these encouraging signs. In the meantime I joined the local Air Training Corps squadron for pre-service instruction, and taught myself Morse code. I knew I couldn't be a pilot but the other jobs I knew I might have a chance at were wireless operator, bomb aimer or navigator. I eventually chose to be a wireless operator because I'd been told it involved the shortest training course – as it turned out I think it was the longest!'

Len's call-up papers eventually arrived in December 1941, a year after he'd been accepted. He was at work when the papers arrived, but because Orsett was a small place where everyone knew everyone, and his uncle was the postmaster and opened the blue envelope as soon as it came in, the whole village knew all about the call-up long before Len.

'I only found out as I cycled back, when a farm labourer friend joined me and said they were talking about it in the pub at lunchtime!'

He was sent to Padgate near Warrington on 23 December 1942 and, as it was nearly Christmas, did absolutely nothing.

'They fed and housed us and we wandered around in our new uniforms and that was it. After two weeks there I was sent to Blackpool – that's the thing about the forces: they're always sending you somewhere or other and you never really know why.'

At Blackpool Len was assigned to a holding unit and then to Initial Training, but though square-bashing, route-marching and daily parades on the seafront followed, there was still little sign of aircrew training.

'I thought we'd never get going. Then I began to have lessons in electricity and magnetism and Morse code for about an hour a day, and every Friday we were given a test. You had to progress from knowing four words of Morse in your first week through six words the following week and so on, until you passed out able to do fourteen words a minute. If you failed one of those Friday exams they put you back a week; if you failed three times you were off the course. Out of forty-nine in my intake only nineteen finished the course and qualified as wireless operators. With Morse you either had a feel for it or you didn't, and of course Morse was absolutely central to a wireless operator's job in those days because there was no other means of communication from a plane.'

Len's next posting on what must at times have seemed an almost endless merry-go-round was to wireless training school at Yatesbury in Wiltshire, where things became slightly more difficult.

LEN REDDINGTON

154

'As well as further Morse code practice – up to eighteen words per minute – we studied electrical theory, communications procedure, wireless tele-phony and radio-telephony. Now, radio-telephony – using a radio for voice communication – was still quite futuristic at this time, but we learned what there was to know about it.

'We were using radios to send our Morse signals but the basic technology was much older – in Victorian times they'd used it to send messages along a wire.'

As well as learning how to send signals, Len was taught how to maintain and repair his radio set. As he explains, this was vital: 'If you had a problem you had to know how to fix it yourself, because in an aeroplane there was no one else to help you.'

Compared with modern communications equipment, the radio sets used by Len and his colleagues now look like cumbersome antiques, but you needed a lot of technical and engineering know-how to use them. It wasn't just a question of flicking a switch and looking at a reading.

'Some of our radio sets were crystal controlled, which meant – without getting too technical – they already had a basic frequency. You then used the circuitry in the radio to double or triple the frequency according to what you needed. You might need to change the frequency because of distance or weather conditions. Some wireless sets didn't have a crystal and these relied on circuitry only. Again, it all sounds a bit complicated – and it was! – but the basic idea was that you used condensers and coils to tune this kind of radio.

'The really early sets that were used on ships had what were called spark transmitters. They literally produced an electrical spark that was audible; but you couldn't have sparks on an aircraft, for obvious reasons! When the thermionic valve was perfected in the 1920s it became possible to put radio sets on aircraft, because the new valve didn't produce dangerous sparks. The thermionic valve was the predecessor of the transistor. It was basically like a valve in an old TV set. When current was applied to it, the heat generated would assist the transmission of the electrodes and amplify the signal.

'The first radio sets I worked on were very primitive. You had a box of coils for the transmitter and a box of coils for the receiver. You would switch the coils about to get the signal you wanted which, as you can imagine, was a damned nuisance. But it was all you had to get your message across. We also had a long wire aerial which was trailed out behind the aircraft, and you had to remember to wind it in before landing!'

The difficulties of these early cumbersome systems can be judged by

one incident that seems amusing now but at the time could have been highly dangerous. 'I remember flying with an instructor and a pupil pilot in an Oxford trainer' (a twin-engined aircraft made by the Airspeed company that was similar to the Anson) 'when the pupil was told to practise recovery from stalling at 8000 feet. He duly stalled the aircraft, but he was too slow in taking the recovery procedure and the plane flipped over and went into a flat spin. We were falling so fast that we all became weightless, along with everything that wasn't fastened down. My battery of accumulators was floating around releasing acid. That was fine while we were floating, but as soon as the instructor gained control of the plane and resumed normal flight we had acid splashed all over everything!'

After his final training, Len qualified as a ground wireless operator. He still wasn't flying, but with every new training course the prospect of taking to the air grew closer.

'I didn't mind a bit that I was to work as a ground-based operator for a while. People forget that if there was a wireless operator in the air there had to be one on the ground as well. It was still 1942 and I was sent – on the move again! – to Tern Hill in Shropshire for six months' practical experience before moving on to air wireless operation. I spent two weeks soldering bits of wire – not quite what I'd expected, but later I was transferred to Calverley in Cheshire as part of a team servicing the equipment on a little trainer aircraft called a Miles Master. This was fitted with a radio telephone set and an ILS radar device which was extremely hush-hush. It was pretty basic but identified the aircraft as friendly. In fact it was so hush-hush that it was fitted with a self-destruct device in case anyone tampered with it!'

Len's seemingly endless series of postings continued when he was sent to Watton in Norfolk and then on to Shawbury in Shropshire. Here fate took a hand and he bumped into a squadron leader in need of a wireless operator. At last the procession of training courses looked as if it might come to an end.

'The squadron leader just walked up to me and said, "Ah, you're just the chap I've been waiting for." I told him I'd never really worked as a WO in an aeroplane, but he just told me not to worry about it. He sent me straight off to get a flying suit, helmet, parachute and headphones. That same afternoon I flew circuits and bumps, but I was so well trained and familiar with the radio equipment that it was easy.'

Over the next six months Len clocked up 200 flying hours. He was now working with an Advanced Flying Unit, as he explains.

'We were training pilots to fly Oxfords and Ansons and my job was to

make sure they didn't get lost. Wherever we flew I kept in touch with base stations and any other stations we passed. You couldn't send a signal and then relax for half an hour. You were constantly sending signals or taking your bearings from radio-direction-finding stations. You also had to get permission from the ground whenever you wanted to change your frequency – you might want to change if, for example, you changed direction.

'As part of our flying training we had to pretend we were landing in thick fog and fly in blind, with the cockpit windows blacked out, using only the radio to land. This was quite an art. You would signal and ask for what was called a QDM approach. If that was OK they'd give you clearance and an initial bearing so you knew where you were in relation to the station. They would then give you a course. They'd send you round the airfield in circuits and you'd try a downwind approach and then a crosswind approach before making your descent. If you'd done everything by the book you would find the runway right in front of you. Later on when I was flying for BOAC I once did all this in thick fog – absolutely nil visibility and we landed just where we needed to be. On that day it was so foggy that we had to get our bearings once we were on the ground just to taxi to the parking area!'

After Shawbury and that glimpse of active service, Len was sent to London for his official flying training.

'While I was there, I was sent to a specialist in London's Wigmore Street who kitted me out with two expensive pairs of glasses – a pair with dark blue lenses for daytime and a pair with light blue lenses for night work. As it turned out I never wore them – they always sat on top of my helmet!'

By this stage he is the first to admit that he was probably over-trained, but at least it meant he sailed through the exams. If he thought his training must at last be over, though, he was mistaken: he was sent back to Yatesbury, where he was to fly on Rapide biplanes.

'There would be about five trainee wireless operators, each with his own radio equipment, in this little plane. The wireless operator sat in a Lloyd Loom chair – the sort of wickerwork chair you might have in a bedroom – that had been bolted to the floor. After that there was flying in a Percival Proctor, just the pilot and one trainee wireless operator.' On completing this course, Len was promoted to sergeant. 'Then I was sent for advanced training on Ansons at Bishops Court in Northern Ireland, but I was so well qualified by now that the chief instructor said it was a waste of time and asked me to be an instructor!

'I did that for a bit and then, in 1943, I was sent to Bramcote in Coventry,

LEN REDDINGTON

158

which was an operations training unit. Here I was supposed to find or become part of a crew. I have to say I didn't like the look of any of the others! But eventually I met an elderly pilot and we got on well; we found a navigator and began flying on Wellington bombers that had been converted for training. The aircraft were old and in poor condition, and sadly a number of the people on the course were killed as a result.

'It was about this time that I first came across wireless radios made by the Americans – after our equipment they were a revelation. The first American radio set I used had a silky-smooth electric motor – it was superb after the old ones I was used to which had been run on old vacuum-cleaner motors! The American machine's main transmitter also had a better coil with a really powerful output.'

At the end of all those months of training, and just when he expected to fly in an operations unit, Len was transferred to the national airline, BOAC. The Corporation had been allocated on Lend-Lease some Consolidated Liberators and Douglas Dakota machines to replace aircraft lost in war service and to help extend civil air routes, and was short of personnel to fly them.

'To be honest, the six crews who were told they were being transferred didn't really want to go! But we had no choice.' Len and his crew were granted leave and told to report to BOAC headquarters, which during the war were in the Grand Spa Hotel at Clifton, Bristol (now the Avon Gorge Hotel). 'It was now near the end of 1943 and five days after arriving at BOAC's HQ in Bristol I handed in my RAF gear and that was that. I was given £70 – a lot of money in those days – and ninety-four clothing coupons for some civvies, and told to get a passport.

'I was measured up for my uniform at BOAC – a lightweight khaki suit for summer and tropical wear, and a double-breasted blue naval officer's uniform for winter. I went to Croydon for another training course! Two months on the special nature of civilian passenger flying, and I was then sent back to Bristol to fly on Dakotas. Despite all my training, I have to say that the standards for civilian flying were actually higher than they were in the RAF – we had to reach eighteen words of Morse per minute but BOAC wanted twenty-five.'

Len began his civilian flying career at Whitchurch Airport near Bristol, but also worked at Croydon – which was still primitive to say the least, as he recalls.

'In 1943 Croydon was all grass fields that hadn't even been levelled! There was a famous hump in the middle of the bit we used as a runway. You went uphill to the bump then down the other side before – hopefully! – taking to

Transatlantic mail about to leave the UK.   IWM CH 11918

the air. But we mostly flew from Bristol because Croydon was by then used only by the BOAC maintenance people.

'The Dakota wasn't such a bad plane for passengers, though of course nothing like as comfortable as today's planes. The fuselage was padded, which reduced noise and made it at least a bit more comfortable-looking. A pair of rails ran down each side of the fuselage floor and onto those were bolted metal-framed seats covered in green canvas. The seats were also pneumatic, so you had a reasonably comfortable ride on your cushion of air. We carried a maximum of twenty-eight passengers but more usually just a dozen or thereabouts. With a dozen we could take out all the seats behind the passengers and fill the gap with freight.

'I also flew for a while on Liberators from Lyneham in Oxfordshire – in those the passengers just had to sit on the floor at the back of the plane. They were fast planes but very uncomfortable for the passengers. Churchill flew in one.'

Len's Dakota days took him regularly from Bristol to Lisbon and then on to Gibraltar and Rabat in Morocco. The Whitchurch runway was only 1000 yards long – which wasn't enough for a fully laden Dakota, so the planes took off with less than a full load of fuel and then landed again at St Mawgan in Cornwall to pick up more fuel. 'St Mawgan had a much longer runway, which meant taking off fully laden was fine – the problems began when we were in the air! Because the war was still on it could take ages to get, for example, to Gibraltar. A journey that should have taken three or four hours once took us ten hours and forty-five minutes! A lot of that had to do with dodging the Germans, of course.

'Later on, all passenger departures were made from Hurn Airport, near Bournemouth, though the aircraft were still based at Whitchurch and serviced there. That procedure went on until London Airport became operational, in 1946.

'In my early days with BOAC we flew Herbert Morrison, the Foreign Minister, as well as J. Arthur Rank of Rank films. The funniest incident we ever had with a passenger involved a Scotsman in a kilt – we flew him to Portugal and then had to fly him back because the authorities wouldn't let him in wearing a dress, as they put it. They said it was against their laws and no amount of persuasion would convince them it wasn't a dress. Leslie Howard the actor was killed in one of our planes, shot down by the Germans. After that incident we only flew at night.'

Len admits that his reservations about moving from the RAF to BOAC were quickly dispelled. After the austerity of RAF stations, some aspects at least of civilian passenger flying were very attractive.

'Being a wireless operator on civilian aircraft was very different from my old RAF days. For a start we got to stay in very good hotels all over the place.

WIRELESS OP.

The control office at Prestwick airport.

LEN REDDINGTON

162

The work was pretty similar, however. We were still the eyes and ears of the plane.

'I flew from Bristol till the end of 1944 and then went to Leuchars in Scotland, flying to Stockholm and Helsinki. We were transporting important business people and government officials, carrying prisoner-of-war mail to and from Germany, repatriating escapees – and bringing in ball bearings imported from Sweden; they were needed for railways and for general manufacturing.

'I was still flying on Dakotas but occasionally also on a Mosquito fighter. If we needed to get a passenger on board the Mosquito we'd put him in the bomb bay! We had to put our ambassador in there once.' The poor passenger, given an eiderdown to wrap himself in and a flask of coffee, had to endure an utterly freezing flight. Len's radio sets were still pretty basic but it was American equipment and there were few significant improvements before the war ended. With hostilities over Len was posted back to Whitchurch, flying to European capitals and to Cairo, Nairobi and Karachi.

'For a wireless operator, overseas work could be tricky, although by now English was becoming the accepted international language. There had been several international conferences to decide on this – previously French had been the international language for airlines.

'To some extent, of course, command of English didn't come into it for the wireless operator. So long as the operator on the ground knew the same

More B.O.A.C. world-famed
Constellations
along **all routes east**!

★ MIDDLE EAST
★ SOUTH AFRICA
★ FAR EAST
★ AUSTRALIA

Limited passenger
list ensures more room
comfort,
personal service!

Fly First Class to the east by B.O.A.C. *Constellation!* Speed! Luxury! Dependability! And *such* luxury, too. Relax—really relax—in the deep comfort of a fully-reclining " slumberseat " . . . a seat where you can s-t-r-e-t-c-h out and sleep soundly, then sit up and just *lounge* in the daytime! Delicious complimentary meals and attentive service throughout your journey. No tips or extras. It's air travel to the east at its best by B.O.A.C. *Constellation.*

Also Tourist services throughout the eastern hemisphere by B.O.A.C. *Argonaut* airliners. Four-engined and fully-pressurized. Same high standard of B.O.A.C. service and experience.

Now in service!		Soon in service!	
To:BANGKOK	JOHANNESBURG	To:ABADAN	DUSSELDORF
BEIRUT	KARACHI	BAGHDAD	HONG KONG
BOMBAY	KHARTOUM	BAHRAIN	KUWAIT
CAIRO	NAIROBI	BASRA	LIVINGSTONE
CALCUTTA	ROME	DAMASCUS	RANGOON
COLOMBO	SINGAPORE	DELHI	TOKYO
DARWIN	SYDNEY	*(Services to South Africa in association with S.A.A.; to Australia in association with Qantas).*	
FRANKFURT	ZURICH		
JAKARTA			

B.O.A.C. TAKES GOOD CARE OF YOU

Consult your local B.O.A.C. Appointed Agent or B.O.A.C., Airways Terminal, Victoria, S.W.1 (VIC 2323); 75 Regent St., W.1 (MAY 6611); or offices in Glasgow, Manchester, Birmingham and Liverpool (see your Telephone Directory for details).

FLY ➤ B·O·A·C

WIRELESS OP.

163

code, we were fine. We used the Q code, a three-letter code with some 200 combinations. For example, QDM meant, "What is the bearing from me to your station?"'

BOAC left Whitchurch at the end of 1948, by which time Len was the flight radio officer in charge there. This was a time of rapid change generally

PLAYER'S CIGARETTES

BRANIFF AIRWAYS: LOCKHEED "ELECTRA"

as, with the war over, scientific and engineering effort could be channelled away from armaments into improving aeroplanes and the equipment used to keep them in the air.

'Everything began to change and by the end of the 1940s BOAC had moved to London Airport. At that time Heathrow was incredibly primitive. They only had tents for the staff and customs people, although there were tarmac runways. The tents were replaced gradually by wooden huts, each hut fitted with a pot-bellied stove to keep the occupants warm. In the severe winter of 1947 the little snow-covered huts with smoke rising from their chimneys looked like something from Santa's grotto, not Britain's number one airport!

'Curiously, when more solid buildings began to go up one was lit by gas until well into the 1950s. The reason was that the building belonged to British Rail and all rail stations were still at that time lit by gas, because in return for the contract to move coal around the country British Rail had to continue to use gas for lighting.'

LEN REDDINGTON

164

When Whitchurch closed Len was transferred to the line operating the transatlantic, Caribbean and Australian services. After a short conversion course onto the Lockheed Constellation 749 – 'a magnificent aeroplane,' he recalls – he spent the next four years flying the Australian route, a return trip that took twenty-one days for the crews.

'The Constellation 749s were bought by BOAC from the Irish airline Aer Lingus. I understand the price for each machine was around £315,000, the highest figure BOAC had ever paid for an aircraft – it sounds like peanuts compared with today's prices.

'All this time the wireless operator's equipment was improving but the basics of the job remained the same. Radio began to come in now and we had VHF transmitters that gave us a range for voice communication of about 120 miles. We used Morse until we were within this range of the airport and then switched to voice.

'Being able to talk to the controller did make it a lot easier, which was just as well because the air was getting crowded. Flying into New York airport using wireless telegraphy at this time would have been impossible. The only problem with the new radio voice contact was that it really was important that everyone spoke good English. Radio contact flying into Lisbon was really difficult, for example, because the ground operators there spoke poor English.'

In 1953 Len was transferred to the Stratocruiser fleet. The Stratocruisers represented a major change in air travel. 'They had Wright Cyclone engines,' recalls Len. 'This was still basically a piston engine, but very powerful, and very comfortable for the passengers. The high cost of flying then can be judged by the fact that it cost £800 for a one-way ticket to Australia – far more than it costs now to go there and back!

'In 1956 I went back onto Constellations on the Far East route and to West Africa, and in 1957 I was transferred to the Canadair Argonaut. But at the end of 1957 satellites began to operate and wireless operators became obsolete. It was a sad day because we'd been a vital part of flying and wireless operation was an enormously skilled business. The Far East line was the first to drop its wireless operators and by 1958, when I was made redundant, nearly all WOs had gone. I was highly qualified but for a trade that was no longer of any use, so in the end I went into my wife's family business – the wine trade.'

Thinking back on his career in flying, Len remembers encounters with many of the pioneers of civil aviation, such as Captains Alcock, Loraine and O. P. Jones, the early Imperial Airways pilots, and Hans Christian Moll, 'The flying Dutchman'. He also recalls many famous passengers on his aircraft, including Douglas Bader, film stars Elizabeth Taylor, Richard Todd and Stewart Grainger, and the cricketer Denis Compton.

'The old wireless equipment exists now in a few museums and every year fewer people are alive who remember how to use it, but that's the way the world works, I suppose.'

TAFFY BARROW
PILOT

When he became a commercial pilot Taffy Barrow once had to tie up one of his passengers – and the passenger in question was no ordinary mortal: he was in fact the Aga Khan. But the whole adventure of becoming a pilot must have seemed an impossible dream for the young man who grew up in rural South Wales in the 1920s. Taffy was born in 1921, and like so many airmen of his generation he would almost certainly have stayed quietly at home but for World War II. True, he developed a passion for the idea of flying as a child, but his parents were dead against the whole idea and it would have been impossible at that time anyway, as flying was a rich man's hobby. As it turned out the war had been on for over a year when, rather than wait to be called up, Taffy persuaded his parents that he should be allowed to join up.

'I joined up in the year of Pearl Harbor. I was twenty and I was only allowed to apply to the Air Force in the end because I'd made a pact with my parents that I wouldn't join up at all unless there was a war. I remember I applied in writing and was called to Oxford for an interview. After just one day I was accepted as what we used to call a pilot under training. I remember that a major part of the selection process was an intelligence test and a series of medicals. I had matriculated from school and I think that was important – they definitely wanted what we used to call School Certificate.

'But anyway, they told me there and then that I was in. To be honest I wasn't interested in the war – I just wanted to fly. The war was a bit of a sideshow so far as I was concerned. I had my interview for the Air Force in March and was told to report in July. This was 1941 and I was part of the first new intake at Lords' Cricket Ground in St John's Wood, North London. We were there to be turned into pilots or navigators.'

This page and opposite: a young Taffy Barrow during wartime training.

Taffy spent two weeks at St John's Wood being kitted out with his uniform, drilled and made to do all kinds of physical training exercises. The candidates were fed at the zoo cafeteria and billeted in luxury flats – stripped of their furnishings. There were also further tests. For pilots they wanted people with really good night vision. To test for night vision potential pilots were fitted with a special collar that stopped movement of the head.

'With this contraption on we had to identify a series of lights shown to us in the dark. I didn't have any problems but some did.'

Having been knocked into shape in London Taffy was sent down to Torquay in Devon.

'This was what we called ground school, where we learned everything from how to identify different aircraft to Morse code and navigation. We were at Torquay for three months. Then after a short period of leave we were put on a troopship to Canada. You have to remember that at this time most of us young men had never been anywhere – and suddenly we were off to the other side of the world.'

The troopship took them to a reception centre at Moncton in New Brunswick. From here they were sent by train to the USA.

'I arrived on Pearl Harbor Day, and went first to Detroit where we were graded after ten hours' flying. If you couldn't fly solo after ten hours you were out. This ten-hour business was US Navy standard procedure for new pilots –

today it probably sounds like an incredibly short space of time in which to make a decision about a new pilot. But this was wartime and I suppose they didn't have the luxury of time to take you through it at a gentler pace.

'Having got through the ten-hour test we were sent to a naval base at Pensacola, Florida. This is where our serious flying training began. We did a lot of practice landing and taking off, including tricky little exercises like spot landing – where your trainers drew a 100-foot diameter circle and you had to touch down each time in that circle, which is a lot more difficult than it sounds. We also learned to fly accurately in a figure of eight round specially positioned pylons. Then after twenty hours we were again tested. If you failed the test – and you might fail for any number of reasons that wouldn't be discussed with you – you were allowed two follow-up checks before you were out.

'Over half the original 150 trainees in my group failed to get through the course and that, I'm afraid, was the end of their chance of becoming a pilot. There was an appeals procedure but I can only remember the failed men being offered re-training in some other Air Force job.

'We trained incredibly intensively – we did what was called an eight-day week. That meant you worked solidly for seven days and then got the eighth off. Each day you spent the morning, from 6 a.m., in ground school and then flew in the afternoon, or you did it the other way round and flew in the morning before going back to the classroom after lunch. Towards the end of the course we had to learn instrument flying – flying the beam as we used to call it. The technique was to listen to a radio signal and land your plane just using the signal and without any other instruments. We also learned to fly in formation at fixed speeds and in various manoeuvres.'

After months of intensive work Taffy was told it was time for flying boat training. Little did he know what he was letting himself in for.

'They were American consolidated P2Y2s built in the early 1930s and they were nothing less than rust buckets, although they had an honourable history – they'd pioneered passenger flying routes to Honolulu. The problem for us was that they were now too old. They were also incredibly sluggish and slow and very heavy on the controls. They sort of lumbered across the water like a dinosaur.

'We spent about eight weeks flying P2Y2s, taking off and landing on the sea off the Florida coast, and despite their cumbersome feel I still enjoyed flying them. I still had the supreme delight in flying that I'd felt from the very first day of my training. You have to remember, too, that the basics of flying don't vary – what we'd done on the little biplanes we'd been trained on was repeated on the big old P2Y2s. Their response of course was very different, but that was something you just had to get used to. We completed our training on Catalina flying boats – which we were also to fly on operations.'

After eleven months abroad Taffy returned to England. It was August 1942 and he was immediately sent to the navigation school at Harrogate in Yorkshire. Having learned the American way of doing things, he now had to learn the RAF way which was very different. A couple of months later he'd moved again – this time to Bristol to fly Oxfords. 'The idea now was that we should get used to flying in British – unpredictable – weather. Up to then we'd really only known the clear blue skies of the USA, so it was a bit of shock to find that suddenly on occasion you couldn't see a thing out of the cockpit because of pouring rain or thick fog. The Oxford was a pretty basic and unexciting passenger aircraft – it was light with twin engines, and we only had them because the RAF had a lot to spare!'

In early 1943 Taffy was posted to Ireland to an operational training unit near Enniskillen. Here he joined a Catalina flying boat. He was the second pilot and the rest of the crew were Canadian.

'We did a few training exercises in the flying boats and were then sent to collect our very own Catalina, which was going to stay with us during our operational tour. If you were to go back in time and look at us you'd say that we were just a bunch of kids, but kids or no we delivered our flying boat to Ceylon as instructed – a trip which proved to be eventful and exciting.

This luxury hotel
flies the Atlantic
ev<u>er</u>y night!

THE Monarch
LONDON TO NEW YORK OR MONTREAL DIRECT

Save up to £28 . 13 . 0 !

UNTIL 31ST MARCH: New York return £228.12.0 instead of £257.5.0; Montreal return £220.18.0 instead of £248.5.0.

Also luxury "MONARCH" services from London to Cairo via Frankfurt (no off-season fare reduction).

B·O·A·C TAKES GOOD CARE OF YOU

Consult your local B.O.A.C. Appointed Agent or S.O.A.C., Airways Terminal, Victoria, S.W.1 (VIC 2323), 75 Regent St., W.1 (MAY 6811), or offices in Glasgow, Manchester, Birmingham and Liverpool (see your Telephone Directory for details).

FLY BRITISH BY **B·O·A·C**

BRITISH   OVERSEAS   AIRWAYS   CORPORATION

Downstairs lounge, double-decked "MONARCH" Stratocruiser.

Fully-reclining seat for every passenger—courteous night-long service.

Delicious complimentary meals and mealtime drinks.

Foam-soft private berths (slight additional charge) —breakfast in bed, if you wish !

PILOT

171

Half Way Across the Pacific

Of course, the Motor Control is Cutler-Hammer

In this electrical age, Motor Control is ever in the vanguard of civilization's onward march, for electric motors now do the back-breaking work wherever men go. Water must be pumped. Air must be moved. Tools must be turned. The needs of the machine shop, homes or hotel on tiny Wake Island, Mid-Pacific station of the Pan-American Airways, are the same as those in your own home town. . . . Being isolated several *thousand* miles from any help, however, makes people very serious about the choice of Motor

Control. No one likes the inconvenience, the waste of time, or the repair costs of mechanical troubles, but on Wake Island such troubles could become a near-calamity. So the Motor Control for Wake Island, delivered there on one of the earliest trips of the famous China Clipper, is all *genuine* Cutler-Hammer Motor Control.

Cutler-Hammer Motor Control is an outstanding choice wherever the importance of reliable, trouble-free electric motor performance is recognized. Many factories use Cutler-Hammer Motor Control exclusively . . . specify it by name for every motor or motorized machine purchased and refuse to accept any substitute. A majority of all electric motor builders recommend Cutler-Hammer Motor Control. Leading machinery builders feature it as standard equipment. A host of independent electrical wholesalers carry adequate stocks for your convenience. CUTLER-HAMMER, Inc., *Pioneer Manufacturers of Electric Control Apparatus*, 1259 St. Paul Avenue, Milwaukee, Wisconsin.

'I'd flown flying boats before but our captain hadn't. We went via Plymouth and Gibraltar, but running short of fuel en route to Cairo, we landed at a place called Derna to refuel. The next day we stumbled our way to Cairo. After Cairo, we continued to Ceylon via Al Habbaniya, Basra, Karachi and Bombay. My logbook shows that the Plymouth–Ceylon flight was some eighty hours, and we now considered ourselves to be an experienced crew! We became fully operational when we arrived at Ceylon. We patrolled the seas looking for German subs, escorted convoys and searched for survivors from U-boat attacks, but only used our depth charges once – we attacked a whale by mistake!

'We covered the seas as far as the Maldives and to Diego Garcia in the Southern Indian Ocean. We did some odd missions, too, including dropping bags of secret letters on isolated islands in the Indian Ocean.'

By February 1944 Taffy had been promoted to captain commanding his own Catalina. By September of that year he was back in Ireland as an instructor for a short time, before going to Blackpool where he flew trainee navigators. Then in February 1945, completely out of the blue, he was asked to go and work for BOAC – they were short of flying boat pilots.

Taffy's first contract in 1945 provided him with a salary of £450 a year, but he managed to double it because allowances paid to staff for being overseas were generous. 'On VE day I flew straight off to South Africa as a passenger. We were supposed to land on a huge dam, but when we arrived there was insufficient water to land on! We diverted and landed at Durban. I was then sent to Richards Bay in Zululand where there was a lake used for training and where I completed my conversion course onto the C-class Empire flying boat. It was a lovely responsive plane to fly. I was sent out to be the first officer and to get the feel of the route – in those days the first officer was a bit of a dogs-body and pretty much did everything.

'The old Imperial Airways captains I worked for thought of themselves as very grand – as lords of the air, you might say – and they were very conscious of their importance and status. They were also very concerned that the crew should treat them with due respect, but then I suppose their flying careers started in many cases back in the Great War. As soon as we took off the captain would disappear to somewhere more comfortable and you – as first officer – had to fly the plane, monitor all the instruments and so on. You were also first on at five in the morning and last off at night. During night stops the first officer had to sort out any engineering problems because BOAC didn't have engineers based at every stop.

'Take the Durban to Calcutta route, which I flew many times – there were twenty-four stops on that journey and there was no way you could have permanent engineering staff on the ground at all those stops. The cost would have been phenomenal.'

By October 1945 Taffy had been promoted to captain. At last he had his own plane – one of the C-class Empire flying boats. Despite all the flying he did on far more modern planes, he still has enormous affection for the C-class.

'I still think that was one of the nicest of all planes to fly. It really was a lovely old aeroplane and because it had such a short range – three and a half to four hours' flying time at most and no navigator – it meant we always stopped somewhere to sleep at night. It was truly leisurely and luxurious by the standards of later passenger flying. It's difficult to compare prices but flying in those days was incredibly expensive. High costs were inevitable because maintenance costs were high for the planes and there were endless stopovers.'

By 1946 Taffy was flying the Durban–Calcutta route. There were three services a week out of Durban. And at main stations on the route to Calcutta the crew might be relieved by another crew and stop for two or three days while waiting to take over the next plane. Durban to Calcutta and back took five weeks, and in those five weeks pilot and copilot would be at the controls for as much as 220 hours.

'Flying technique on those wonderful old C-class was straightforward, easy and really enjoyable – occasionally taking off in a swell could cause porpoising, a kind of up-and-down motion you had to avoid by pulling the control stick back – and landing was sometimes plagued by crosswinds. To land in a crosswind the technique was to dig the wing in on the upwind side and fly crabwise as it were, almost sideways, and then in the instant before you touched down you would straighten the plane up.

'A lot of people have this idea that you needed the sea to be glass-calm to land a flying boat – in fact we often preferred it if there was a bit of a chop on the water. If the water was as calm as a millpond you would set the instruments to make sure you had a fixed rate of descent – and even then you often didn't notice you were down until long after you'd actually landed!'

Taffy was the very last man to be promoted to captain on those old Empire flying boats. In February 1946 he came home to England and was moved on to Hythe flying boats. All the famous Empire boats were unceremoniously scrapped – even the Science Museum turned down the chance to preserve

Opposite: A crowd gathers by the Nile to watch a BOAC Empire flying boat about to touch down at the marine airport of Rod-el-Farag, Cairo. IWM CH 14071

PAST EXPERIENCE AS A PILOT.

MILITARY.	CIVIL.
Date of Commission 22-2-44	
„ Qualified for Wings 15-7-42	
„ Demobilized	
Highest Rank held	
Decorations Awarded	
Approx. Hours Flown { By Day 1100 / „ Night 300	Approx. Hours Flown { By Day / „ Night
Total Hours Flown on Service 1400	Total Hours Flown as Civilian Pilot

Approx.: Total Flying Time as a Pilot to date = 1400 hours

N

22

NO. 7. COMMAND COURSE. RICHARDS BAY ZULULAND. RECORD OF

Date.	Aircraft.		Engines.		Journey.	
	Type.	Markings.	Type.	H.P.	From.	To.
						Brought forward
						RICHARDS BAY
17.1.46.	S.30.	G. AFKZ CATHAY			DURBAN	
18.1.46.						
19.1.46.						
19.1.46.						
22.1.46.						
22.1.46.						
22.1.46.						
23.1.46.						
						Carried forward

PAST EXPERIENCE—*cont.*

Types Flown.	Hours Flown on each Type.	No. of Accidents.	Remarks.
CATALINA	1050	0	
OXFORD.	40	0	
ANSON	100	0	
KINGFISHER	20	0	
VULTEE VALIANT.	20	0	
HARVARD.	35	0	
N3N	100	0	
P2Y2	30	0	

I CERTIFY that the information on this and the preceding pages is accurate to the best of my knowledge.

Date 11-7-45   Signature of Pilot _____

FLIGHTS.

Time of Departure.		Time of Arrival.		Time in Air.		Pilot. See Instructions (5) & (6) on flyleaf of this book.	Remarks.
Hrs.	Mins.	Hrs.	Mins.	Hrs.	Mins.		
...	...	...	...	350	34		
12	10	13	05		55	CAPT. WOODHOUSE.	
07	40	09	50	2	10		4.9.10.11.12.14.21. GENERAL CHECK DUAL.
05	20	06	00		40		9.10. DUAL.
08	10	09	30	1	20	SELF	9.10.11.12. SOLO.
05	05	06	05	1	00	CAPT. WOODHOUSE	9.10.11.12. LANDING VARYING FLAP DUAL.
08	00	10	00	2	00	SELF	9.10.11.12. SOLO.
12	20	13	10		50	,,	9.10.11.12. 7/0 VARYING FLAP.
08	00	08	30		30	CAPT. WOODHOUSE	GLASSY TAKEOFFS + LANDINGS
...	...	...	...	360	09		

177

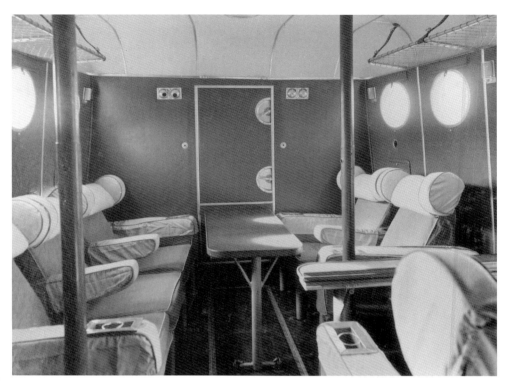
The interior of a flying boat.

one on the grounds that it didn't have the space to store it. The Hythe was the civilian equivalent of the old Sunderland flying boat and big brother to the old Empires.

'I flew Hythes to Australia and the Far East. They had a much longer range than the C-class – in fact where the C-class could do three and a half to four hours' flying the Hythe could do seven to eight hours. The days of flying in a leisurely manner with no navigator were well and truly over. We had engineers and navigators on board too, so we flew at night. It was all very different from flying the C-class flying boats. We had a lot more passengers to worry about, apart from anything else – most were civil servants and army people.

'The Aga Khan was once one of our passengers and he caused us a few problems. He was so big that we couldn't get the safety belt round him. The rules said that we couldn't land or take off if the passengers were not all strapped in, so to get round the problem we borrowed a length of webbing that would normally be used for freight and we tied the Aga Khan in with that! He then got in a bit of a panic because he wanted to know how he would untie himself quickly in the event of an emergency. We had to think about that one, but then the solution came to us: we gave him a carving knife from the galley and told him that if there was a problem he could cut his way out! Somehow I don't think we'd get away with that today.

'But I should point out that although we were now a little less leisurely than we'd been in the C-class days we were still luxurious in comparison to more recent times. There was masses of room for passengers to move about, for example, because seats were still arranged round tables rather than in tight rows as they are now.

'The Hythes had been around since the early part of the war, but they were still in a sense a sort of grown-up version of the old C-class. They were much heavier with more powerful engines. There was also the Plymouth version of the Hythe, which differed only in that it had American-built engines. Most of the other pilots from those early BOAC days were ex-RAF like me, with just a sprinkling of pre-war Imperial Airways staff who'd probably started their careers during World War I or just after.

'Flying boats moved from Poole to Southampton in 1948. It was considered more convenient and they'd built a special-purpose terminal by now – the terminal was fitted out with a winch that was used to tow the plane in on a wire from the buoy. This meant they could do away with launches.'

The flying boats finished abruptly in 1950, but Taffy had already left to fly Lockheed Constellations. These four-engined land-planes were quite different from the flying boats – the major difference from a pilot's point of view was that they had power controls and, of course, an undercarriage.

'That took some getting used to – it was years since I'd had an undercarriage to deal with, and compared to landing on the sea with a flying boat a runway looked very much like a postage stamp to me!

'I re-trained at a place called Filton, near Bristol, for three or four months. Then I began flying a Constellation on the mid-Atlantic route down through the Azores, Havana, Jamaica and Antigua Bay. After two years BOAC started what was called a coach service on the North Atlantic – for the first time they introduced what was called first tourist class rather than first class. But flying was still an expensive luxury, and even with the extremely high prices BOAC couldn't make a profit and they were subsidized by government. The introduction of jet engines didn't just change the pace of flying. They also led eventually to a great reduction in cost because they were so much faster and less expensive to maintain than the old piston engines.

'Constellations were around until 1954–55, when they were phased out and I was moved to the Stratocruiser. Now this was an interesting plane – it was the first I'd flown that had a pressurized cabin and compared to the flying

boats and the Constellations it was a big plane. It was also very awkward to land. People used to say that piloting a Stratocruiser was like sitting on a chimney and flying a house. Mind you, if it was difficult to fly it was at the same time very well kitted out – it carried eighty passengers and even had bunk beds

so they could have a sleep. It was made by Boeing and had a number of new high-tech navigational devices and other technical improvements.

'After Stratocruisers I flew long-range Britannias, but as the planes became more sophisticated, with power controls and increasingly advanced autopilots, flying them became very monotonous. As pilot you were very much just a watcher – by which I mean you kept an eye on your instruments and apart from that had very little to do.

'The Britannia was unusual in that it was a propjet – a sort of hybrid if you like, between the old world of flying and the new. I flew Britannias from London to New York and the propjet idea was that the jet part of the engine was used to drive the prop. At the time it was thought that this system would be more economic than just using a jet engine. It was an idea that was quickly rejected. Mind you, having said that, I know that the last Britannia was still flying in 2001.'

Taffy never flew Comets but by 1964 he was flying the aeroplane that replaced them – the VC10.

'Of course jet engines changed the whole feel of flying – ironically, given that they were so new and revolutionary, they were much slower to respond than a prop-driven plane unless you turned a lot of power on. With a prop the response is immediate, but of course the big thing with jets was that they could fly much faster and much higher. The 747 was and is a great plane – despite its size it had incredibly light controls, because they were power controlled. I flew them from 1970 to 1975 when I had to stop flying because I failed a medical. Since then I've been up in a flying boat with the actress Maureen O'Hara's husband! He bought one of the last flying boats to fly her home to Ireland from America. When I flew with them I realized how much I'd forgotten – the noise and vibration were incredible!'

PICTURE CREDITS
AND ACKNOWLEDGEMENTS

Extract from *Venture to the Interior* by Laurens van der Post, published by Chatto and Windus, used by permission of The Random House Group Limited.

Extract from *A Life in Movies* by Michael Powell used by permission of Faber and Faber Ltd.

PICTURE CREDITS:

The Advertising Archives: ii, v, 2, 11, 13, 16, 21, 24, 28, 32, 39, 44, 48, 49, 51, 61, 64, 68, 73, 101, 104, 108, 120, 121, 122, 129, 132, 133, 136, 137, 141, 149, 152, 153, 156, 163, 171, 172, 180.
Imperial War Museum: 1, 10 (top), 29, 46, 57, 58-9, 63, 99, 103 (top and bottom), 111, 124, 125, 126, 127, 130, 135, 139, 143, 145, 147, 160, 162, 166, 175.
Science and Society Picture Library: 3, 6, 7, 8, 9, 10 (bottom), 54, 117.
Ron Ballantine: 4, 14, 17.
David Rose: 18, 20, 22, 23, 26, 27.
Vic Avila, 40, 45.
Ted Williams: 55.
Olive Carlisle: 70, 75, 76, 77, 79, 82, 83, 84, 85, 93, 109.
Ken Emmott: 96, 106, 107.
Hazel Rose: 134, 138.
Len Reddington: 150.
Taffy Barrow: 168, 169, 176-7.
Eric Whitehead Photography: 94-95.

All other photographs by the author.

Thanks to all the retired airline staff who talked to me and to Gillian Kemp, Pam Hunt, Sandie Rose, Phyllis Bennett, Annette Hedges, Jerry Holland, Emma Westall, Jo Davis and Graham Coster at Aurum.

INDEX

GUILDFORD **college**

Learning Resource Centre

Please return on or before the last date shown.
No further issues or renewals if any items are overdue.

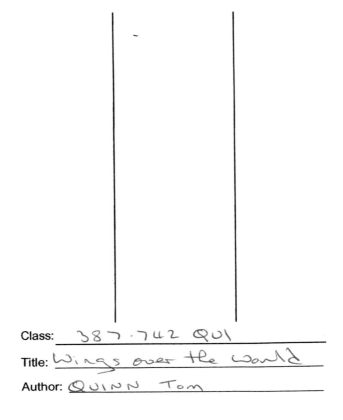

Class: 387.742 QUI

Title: Wings over the World

Author: QUINN Tom